"Walter Brueggemann is a legend. He is one of the most influential biblical scholars of the past century. Few people have inspired me more than Walter, especially as we try to understand what it means to be God's peculiar people in the belly of the empire. This series is sort of like the 'best hits' album of one of the world's greatest theologians."

—Shane Claiborne, author, activist,
and cofounder of Red Letter Christians

"Oh, the bold sermons we will preach, the courageous classes we will teach, and the brave and faithful commentary we will craft with vivid prophetic imagination because of the timely production of this volume of illuminating writings by the inimitable Walter Brueggemann. I savored my review copy, drinking greedily of its wisdom that is essential for these extraordinarily difficult times. You will need this on your shelf, shapers of theological reflection and world-healing action, coming to it again and again to deliver yourself from stale theologies and to liberate God—and hope—for a generation desperately needing to know the true heart of the One who frees us to flourish in community. This is a banquet of rich exegesis and exposition that equips us to heal the world."

—Jacqui Lewis, author, activist, preacher, and Senior
Minister for Public Theology and Transformation,
Middle Church, New York City

"The exodus story has always fascinated me. It is, at once, powerful and complicated—a resource for liberation and for imagining a different, more just way of living in the world. Reading Walter Brueggemann's *Deliver Us*, especially in these dark times, is an exhilarating experience. In his hands, the exodus story boldly speaks to our troubles. Brilliance and an abiding commitment to a more merciful and just social order jump from the page."

—Eddie S. Glaude Jr., James S. McDonnell Distinguished
University Professor, Princeton University

Deliver Us

The Walter Brueggemann Library

Davis Hankins, *Editor*

Deliver Us

Salvation and the Liberating God
of the Bible

Walter Brueggemann

WESTMINSTER
JOHN KNOX PRESS
LOUISVILLE • KENTUCKY

First edition
Published by Westminster John Knox Press
Louisville, Kentucky

22 23 24 25 26 27 28 29 30 31—10 9 8 7 6 5 4 3 2 1

Unless otherwise indicated, Scripture quotations are from the New Revised Standard Version of the Bible, copyright © 1989 by the Division of Christian Education of the National Council of the Churches of Christ in the U.S.A., and are used by permission.

See acknowledgments, pp. 203–4, for additional permission.

Book design by Sharon Adams
Cover design by designpointinc.com

Library of Congress Cataloging-in-Publication Data

Names: Brueggemann, Walter, author. | Hankins, Davis, editor.
Title: Deliver us : salvation and the liberating God of the Bible / Walter Brueggemann.
Description: First edition. | Louisville, Kentucky : Westminster John Knox Press, [2022] | Series: The Walter Brueggemann library ; vol. 1 | Summary: "Examines the narrative of Exodus through Brueggemann's numerous publications in recent decades, making clear that divine liberation from exploitation and acquisitiveness also means liberation for generous action for the common good"-- Provided by publisher.
Identifiers: LCCN 2022028734 (print) | LCCN 2022028735 (ebook) | ISBN 9780664265885 (paperback) | ISBN 9781646982783 (ebook)
Subjects: LCSH: Bible. Exodus--Criticism, interpretation, etc. | Salvation--Biblical teaching.
Classification: LCC BS1245.6.S25 B78 2022 (print) | LCC BS1245.6.S25 (ebook) | DDC 222.1206--dc23/eng/20220808
LC record available at https://lccn.loc.gov/2022028734
LC ebook record available at https://lccn.loc.gov/2022028735

Most Westminster John Knox Press books are available at special quantity discounts when purchased in bulk by corporations, organizations, and special-interest groups. For more information, please e-mail SpecialSales@wjkbooks.com.

For David and Peter Knauert, of blessed memory

Contents

Series Preface

I have been very pleased that David Dobson and his staff at Westminster John Knox Press have proposed this extended series of republications of my work. Indeed, I know of no old person who is not pleased to be taken seriously in old age! My first thought, in learning of this proposed series, is that my life and my work have been providentially fortunate in having good companions all along the way who have both supported me and for the most part kept me honest in my work. I have been blessed by the best teachers, who have prepared me to think both critically and generatively I have been fortunate to be accompanied by good colleagues, both academic and pastoral, who have engaged my work. And I have been gifted to have uncommonly able students, some of whom continue to instruct me in the high art of Old Testament study.

The long years of my work that will be represented in this series reflect my slow process of finding my own voice, of sorting out accents and emphases, and of centering my work on recurring themes that I have judged to merit continuing attention. The result of that slow process is that over time my work is marked by repetition and reiteration, as well as contradiction, change of mind, and ambiguity, all of which belongs to seeing my work as an organic whole as I have been given courage and insight. In the end I have settled on recurring themes (reflected in the organization of this series) that I hope I have continued to treat with imagination, so that my return to them is not simply reiteration but is critically generative of new perspective and possibility.

In retrospect, I can identify two learnings from the philosopher and hermeneut Paul Ricoeur that illumine my work. Ricoeur has given me names for what I have been doing, even though I was at work on such matters before I acquired Ricoeur's terminology. First, in his book *Freud and Philosophy* (1965), Ricoeur identifies two moves that are essential for interpretation. On the one hand there is "suspicion." By this term Ricoeur means critical skepticism. In biblical study "suspicion" has taken the form of historical criticism, in which the interpreter doubts the "fictive" location and function of the text and hypothesizes about the "real, historical" location and function of the text. On the other hand, there is "retrieval," by which Ricoeur means the capacity to reclaim what is true in the text after due "suspicion." My own work has included measures of "suspicion," because a grounding in historical criticism has been indispensable for responsible interpretation. My work, however, is very much and increasingly tilted toward "retrieval," the recovery of what is theologically urgent in the text. My own location in a liberal-progressive trajectory of interpretation has led me to an awareness that liberal-progressives are tempted to discard "the baby" along with "the bath." For that reason, my work has been to recover and reclaim, I hope in generative imaginative ways, the claims of biblical faith.

Second and closely related, Ricoeur has often worked with a grid of "precritical/critical/postcritical" interpretation. My own schooling and that of my companions has been in a critical tradition; that enterprise by itself, however, has left the church with little to preach, teach, or trust. For that reason, my work has become increasingly postcritical, that is, with a "second naiveté," a readiness to engage in serious ways the claims of the text. I have done so in a conviction that the alternative metanarratives available to us are inadequate and the core claims of the Bible are more adequate for a life of responsible well-being. Both liberal-progressive Christians and fundamentalist Christians are tempted and seduced by alternative narratives that are elementally inimical to the claims of the Bible; for that reason, the work of a generative exposition of biblical claims seems to me urgent. Thus I anticipate that this series may be a continuing invitation to the ongoing urgent work of exposition that both makes clear the singular claims of the Bible and exposes the inadequacy of competing narratives that, from a biblical perspective, amount to idolatry. It is my hope that such continuing work will not only give preachers something substantive to preach and give teachers something substantive to teach, but will invite the church to embrace the biblical claims that it can "trust and obey."

My work has been consistently in response to the several unfolding crises facing our society and, more particularly, the crises faced by the church. Strong market forces and ideological passions that occupy center stage among us sore tempt the church to skew its tradition, to compromise its gospel claim, and to want to be "like the nations" (see 1 Sam. 8:5, 20), that is, without the embarrassment of gospel disjunction. Consequently I have concluded, over time, that our interpretive work must be more radical in its awareness that the claims of faith increasingly contradict the dominant ideologies of our time. That increasing awareness of contradiction is ill-served by progressive-liberal accommodation to capitalist interests and, conversely, it is ill-served by the packaged reductions of reactionary conservatism. The work we have now to do is more complex and more demanding than either progressive-liberal or reactionary-conservative offers. Thus our work is to continue to probe this normative tradition that is entrusted to us that is elusive in its articulation and that hosts a Holy Agent who runs beyond our explanatory categories in irascible freedom and in bottomless fidelity.

I am grateful to the folk at Westminster John Knox and to a host of colleagues who continue to engage my work. I am profoundly grateful to Davis Hankins, on the one hand, for his willingness to do the arduous work of editing this series. On the other hand, I am grateful to Davis for being my conversation partner over time in ways that have evoked some of my better work and that have fueled my imagination in fresh directions. I dare anticipate that this coming series of republication will, in generative ways beyond my ken, continue to engage a rising generation of interpreters in bold, courageous, and glad obedience.

Walter Brueggemann

Editor's Introduction

I began theological education just as Walter Brueggemann was scheduled to retire at Columbia Theological Seminary. I knew very little about the academic study of religion, probably even less about the state of biblical scholarship at the turn of the twenty-first century, yet somehow I knew enough to take every possible course with Dr. Brueggemann. After retiring, Walter continued to teach a course periodically and work from his study on campus—and he always insisted that it and any pastor's work space be called a "study" rather than an "office"! But before he retired, during his last and my first year at Columbia, I took six different courses in biblical studies, including three with Walter. In my memory, I spent that academic year much like St. Thecla as she sat in a windowsill and listened to the teachings of the apostle Paul. According to her mother's descriptive flourish, Thecla, "clinging to the window like a spider, lays hold of what is said by him with a strange eagerness and fearful emotion." It was for me as it had been for Thecla.

Longtime readers as well as those encountering Walter's words for the first time will discover in the volumes of the Walter Brueggemann Library the same soaring rhetoric, engaging intelligence, acute social analysis, moral clarity, wit, generosity, and grace that make it so enlightening and enjoyable to learn from and with Walter Brueggemann. The world we inhabit is broken, dominated by the special interests of the wealthy, teeming with misinformation, divided by entrenched social hierarchies, often despairing before looming ecological catastrophe, and callously indifferent, if not aggressively predatory, toward those facing increasing deprivation and immiseration. In these volumes readers will find Walter at his best, sharply naming these dynamics of brokenness and richly engaging biblical traditions to uncover and chart alternative forms of collective life that promise to be more just, more merciful, and more loving.

Each volume in the Walter Brueggemann Library coheres around a distinct theme that is a prominent concern across Walter's many publications. The contents of the volumes consist of materials taken from a variety of his previously published works. In other words, I have compiled whole chapters or articles, sections, snippets, and at times even just a line or two from Walter's publications, and sought to weave them together to create a new book that coheres around a specific theme, in this case the theme of salvation in the biblical traditions. Readers who are familiar with Walter's work will not be surprised that this initial volume centers on his expositions on the event of the exodus as definitive and paradigmatic for the Bible's understanding of salvation. Such experienced readers may also discover that this thematic focus somewhat curtails what Brent Strawn aptly describes as Walter's "canonical dexterity," that is, his unrivaled ability to range freely and broadly across the various genres and sections of the Bible, Old and New Testament alike. My hope is that the gains from this thematic cohesion at least somewhat make up for whatever is lost in canonical dexterity.

The word "salvation" is relatively rare in Brueggemann's publications. He much prefers to speak of liberation, emancipation, restoration, transformation, reconciliation, and the like. This may be a consequence of the baggage carried by the notion of "salvation" or "being saved" in some contemporary streams of Christianity, especially in the United States. But regardless, whenever such salvific ideas appear in Brueggemann's work, he often attends to the broader, more encompassing categories of both gift and task that were so important in the Protestant Reformation and remain so in Jewish and Christian theology more broadly.[1] Brueggemann similarly demonstrates and emphasizes that any conception of salvation rooted in biblical traditions ought to link gift and task. The biblical God characteristically saves people not only *from* certain conditions, but also *for* a full restoration of their well-being.

In these chapters Brueggemann consistently returns to the basic
elements within the book of Exodus, namely, the story of liberation followed by the guidance, stipulations, and laws adopted by the
newly liberated community, first in Egypt, then in the wilderness,
but especially at Mount Sinai. Thus, while the biblical story of the
exodus is a particular narrative, specific to the circumstance of the
Hebrew people in Egypt, it becomes paradigmatic in the Bible for
the gifts and tasks that constitute a range of experiences of salvation.
Whether the people of God find themselves in Egypt, in exile, or
in contemporary settings of neoliberal capitalism, the exodus offers
an archetype through which humans can better grasp the constrain-
ing forces of anxiety, injustice, and exploitation that pose perpetual
threats to the flourishing of life, and imagine and be energized for
new and liberating modes of social organization. The ancient story,
Brueggemann wagers, has the capacity to overcome the fear, despair,
and denial of the reigning dystopian order that views resources as
scarce and all in cutthroat competition for them. Liberation frees the
community to assume the tasks of a more just and more merciful
social order, and respond with joyful gratitude for its newly emancipated future.

In organizing this volume, I have aimed to create some narrative cohesion across four parts. Part 1 focuses on the emancipatory
event of the exodus and the circumstances of anxiety, overproduction, exploitation, and violent oppression in Egypt from which the
Israelites are liberated. Part 2 turns to the tasks announced in the
commandments of the Decalogue, which summon the Israelites,
on the basis of their new faith in the exodus-causing and Sabbath-
observing God, to commit their social order to neighborly engagement for the sake of the common good. The three chapters in part 3
center on other legal materials in the Torah that develop the baseline
obligations in the Decalogue so that the entirety of Israel's social life
would be centered on the creator God who saved them in the exodus
event. Part 4 explores how this covenantal paradigm for salvation
gets inflected in various biblical texts, especially in narrative and
prophetic traditions, and also in the words and life of Jesus. Finally,
a brief conclusion continues a thread running throughout the book:
Brueggemann's ceaseless effort to emphasize the significance of

the biblical paradigm of salvation for contemporary communities of faith, particularly in the context of the church in the United States.

Finally, I would like to express my immense gratitude. First to Walter, for trusting me with this project as with so much, and most especially for the boundless care he has shown me and my family for many years. Also, to the good folks at Westminster John Knox, for conceiving the idea of this series, for their editorial guidance, and their patience through a series of events that caused several delays, including a global pandemic. Finally, I would like to thank my department chair, Kevin Schilbrack, and Dean Neva Specht, for their consistent support and encouragement on this and many other projects.

Davis Hankins
Appalachian State University
Fall 2021

PART ONE

The Liberating Event

Chapter 1

Exodus from Egypt

Emancipation from Anxiety and Exploitation

When we come to the question of salvation in the Bible, the exodus story is unquestionably the indispensable starting point. The exodus narrative provides Israel with a clear paradigm for, first, identifying communal and individual crises, and second, imagining emancipation into an alternative, sustainable way of life. The great crisis for ancient Israel was, as it is for us, a crisis of "the common good," the sense of communal solidarity that binds all in a common destiny—haves and have-nots, rich and poor, Hebrews and Egyptians, Blacks and whites. We face a crisis about the common good because there are powerful forces at work among us to resist the common good, to violate community solidarity, and to deny a common destiny. Mature people, at their best, are people who are committed to the common good that reaches beyond private interests, transcends sectarian commitments, and offers human solidarity.

I

Ancient Israel faces its crisis in the grip of Pharaoh's Egypt. In the Hebrew Bible/Old Testament, ancient Pharaoh is a cipher and metaphor that symbolizes the paradigmatic enemy of the common good, an agent of immense power who could not get beyond his acquisitive interest to ponder the common good. He embodies and represents raw, absolute, worldly power. He is, like Pilate after him, a stand-in for the whole of empire. Pharaoh is an example and an embodiment of a complex system of monopoly that, along with the

3

wealth that it manages, produces anxiety that affects every dimension of the system.

First, regarding the wealth that Pharaoh manages, Egypt was of course the breadbasket of the ancient world. Already in Genesis 12, the very first chapter of Israel in the Old Testament, we learn that Pharaoh had ample food and could supply the entire world:

> Now there was a famine in the land. So Abram went down to Egypt to reside there as an alien, for the famine was severe in the land. (v. 10)

It was natural and automatic that the Nile Valley should produce bread. A need for bread drove Abraham to the place of security and sufficiency.

Second, regarding the anxiety produced by Pharaoh's "empire of force,"[1] there is high irony in the report that Pharaoh, the leader of the superpower, has bad dreams. He might be competent and in control all day long, but when he is asleep at night and his guard is down and his competence is relaxed, he has nightmares. The one with everything has dreams of insecurity:

> Then Pharaoh said to Joseph, "In my dream I was standing on the banks of the Nile; and seven cows, fat and sleek, came up out of the Nile and fed in the reed grass. Then seven other cows came up after them, poor, very ugly, and thin. Never had I seen such ugly ones in all the land of Egypt. The thin and ugly cows ate up the first seven fat cows, but when they had eaten them no one would have known that they had done so, for they were still as ugly as before. Then I awoke. I fell asleep a second time and I saw in my dream seven ears of grain, full and good, growing on one stalk, and seven ears, withered, thin, and blighted by the east wind, sprouting after them; and the thin ears swallowed up the seven good ears." (Gen. 41:17–24)

He is desperate to find out the meaning of the dream; but no one in the intelligence community of his empire can decode the secret message. Finally, as a last resort, he summons an unknown Israelite from prison. According to this ancient narrative, the uncredentialed Israelite can decode what the empire cannot discern. Joseph the interpreter immediately grasps the point. The nightmare is about *scarcity*. The one with everything dreams of *deficiency*. The cows and the shocks of grain anticipate years of famine when no food will be produced.

Pharaoh receives the interpretation of his nightmare and sets about to make imperial policy. As readers of the narrative, we are permitted to watch while the *nightmare* is turned into *policy*. Pharaoh asks for a plan of action, and Joseph, modest man that he is, nominates himself as food czar:

> Now therefore let Pharaoh select a man who is discerning and wise, and set him over the land of Egypt. (v. 33)

Joseph, blessed Israelite that he is, is not only a shrewd dream interpreter; he is, as well, an able administrator who commits himself to Pharaoh's food policy. The royal policy is to accomplish a food monopoly. In that ancient world as in any contemporary world, food is a weapon and a tool of control.

We learn of *policy* rooted in *nightmare* (Gen. 47:13–26). The peasants, having no food of their own, come to Joseph, now a high-ranking Egyptian, and pay their money in exchange for food, so that the centralized government of Pharaoh achieves even greater wealth (v. 14). After the money is all taken, the peasants come again and ask for food. This time Joseph, on behalf of Pharaoh, takes their cattle, what Karl Marx called their "means of production" (vv. 15–17). In the next year, the third year, the peasants still need food. But they have no money and they have no livestock. In the third year they gladly surrender their freedom in exchange for food:

> Shall we die before your eyes, both we and our land? Buy us and our land in exchange for food. We with our land will become slaves to Pharaoh; just give us seed, so that we may live and not die, and that the land may not become desolate. (v. 19)

The narrative knows the way in which hungry peasants, in need of food from the monopoly, will pay their money, then forfeit their cattle, and then finally give up their land, because Pharaoh leverages food in order to enhance his power. In the end, the peasants are so "happy" that they asked to be "owned." And the inevitable outcome:

> So Joseph bought all the land of Egypt for Pharaoh. All the Egyptians sold their fields, because the famine was severe upon them;

and the land became Pharaoh's. As for the people, he made slaves
of them from one end of Egypt to the other. (vv. 20–21)

Slavery in the Old Testament happens because the strong ones
work a monopoly over the weak ones, and eventually exercise control over their bodies. Not only that; in the end the peasants, now
become slaves, are grateful for their dependent status:

They said, "You have saved our lives; may it please my lord, we
will be slaves to Pharaoh." (v. 25)

This is an ominous tale filled with irony, a part of the biblical text we
do not often enough note. We know about the exodus deliverance,
but we do not take notice that slavery occurred by the manipulation
of the economy in the interest of a concentration of wealth and power
for the few at the community's expense. In reading the Joseph narrative we characteristically focus on the providential texts of Genesis
45:1–15 and 50:20, to the neglect of the down-and-dirty narratives
of economic transaction.

From the outset, Pharaoh, blessed by God's Nile, was the leader
of the breadbasket of the world (see Gen. 12:10). By his own actions
and those of his food czar, Joseph, Pharaoh advanced the claims of
the state against his own subjects, achieving a monopoly on land
and on the food supply, which he uses as a weapon against his own
people. That land and food supply became a tax base whereby wealth
was systematically transferred from the peasant-slaves to the central
monopoly. Because Pharaoh has so much food, he needs granaries
in which to store his surplus. The construction of such storehouses
for surplus was the work of those who were forced by famine into
slave labor:

Therefore they set taskmasters over them to oppress them with
forced labor. They built supply cities, Pithom and Rameses, for
Pharaoh. (Exod. 1:11)

The narrative does not miss the irony that those forced by famine
into slavery are engaged in storing the surplus of the empire. It is
astonishing that critical scholarship has asked forever about the identification of these storehouse cities, but without ever asking about the
skewed exploitative social relationships between owner and laborers

that the project exhibits. The storehouse cities are an ancient parallel to the great banks and insurance houses where surplus wealth is kept among us. That surplus wealth, produced by the cheap labor of peasants, must now be protected from the peasants by law and by military force. Pharaoh's great accumulation of wealth—in land and in food—is the outcome of cheap labor. The cunning food administration plans of Joseph have created for Pharaoh a peasant underclass of very cheap labor.

With reference to the common good, we may formulate a tentative conclusion about the narrative of Pharaoh: *Those who are living in anxiety and fear, most especially fear of scarcity, have no time or energy for the common good.* Anxiety is no adequate basis for the common good; anxiety will cause the formulation of policy and exploitative practices that are inimical to the common good, a systemic greediness that precludes the common good.

II

By the end of the book of Genesis, we have a deteriorated social situation consisting in Pharaoh and the state slaves who submit their bodies to slavery in order to receive food from the state monopoly. All parties in this arrangement are beset by anxiety, the slaves because they are exploited, Pharaoh because he is fearful and on guard. The narrative of the book of Exodus is organized into a great contest that is, politically and theologically, an exhibit of the ongoing contest between the *urge to control* and the *power of emancipation* that in ancient Israel is perennially linked to the God of the exodus.

Pharaoh's exploitation of cheap labor is without restraint. He is propelled by insatiable greed. He has more food to store; and so he needs more granaries; and to have more granaries, he must have more bricks out of which they are to be constructed. Thus, Exodus 5 paints a picture of the frantic, aggressive policies of the empire that are propelled by anxiety:

1. First, we learn that the imperial system is a system of raw, ruthless exploitation, always pressing cheap labor for more production

and permitting no slippage or accommodation. Exodus 5 is permeated with harsh pharaonic commands to the cheap labor force, unbearable labor conditions, and unrealistic production schedules:

> But the king of Egypt said to them, "Moses and Aaron, why are you taking the people away from their work? Get to your labors!" (Exod. 5:4)

> That same day Pharaoh commanded the taskmasters of the people, as well as their supervisors, "You shall no longer give the people straw to make bricks, as before; let them go and gather straw for themselves. But you shall require of them the same quantity of bricks as they have made previously; do not diminish it, for they are lazy; that is why they cry, 'Let us go and offer sacrifice to our God.' Let heavier work be laid on them; then they will labor at it and pay no attention to deceptive words." (vv. 6–9)

The supervisors simply carry out the demands of the empire:

> So the taskmasters and the supervisors of the people went out and said to the people, "Thus says Pharaoh, 'I will not give you straw. Go and get straw yourselves, wherever you can find it; but your work will not be lessened in the least.'" (vv. 10–11)

The taskmasters are relentless:

> The taskmasters were urgent, saying, "Complete your work, the same daily assignment as when you were given straw." And the supervisors of the Israelites, whom Pharaoh's taskmasters had set over them, were beaten, and were asked, "Why did you not finish the required quantity of bricks yesterday and today, as you did before?" (vv. 13–14)

Despite the beatings, the Israelite supervisors of labor who have been co-opted and coerced by Pharaoh to make the system work issue a protest to the crown:

> Then the Israelite supervisors came to Pharaoh and cried, "Why do you treat your servants like this? No straw is given to your servants, yet they say to us, 'Make bricks!' Look how your servants are beaten! You are unjust to your own people." (vv. 15–16)

But Pharaoh, the voice of the imperial production system, is relentless:

> He said, "You are lazy, lazy; that is why you say, 'Let us go and sacrifice to the LORD.' Go now, and work; for no straw shall be given you, but you shall still deliver the same number of bricks." (vv. 17–18)

And the supervisors were quick to issue the new ferocious demands to the slave community:

> The Israelite supervisors saw that they were in trouble when they were told, "You shall not lessen your daily number of bricks." (v. 19)

Israel's memory of Egypt's imperial economy is of an irrepressible brick quota and an impossible production schedule. And like any driven production system, the quotas keep increasing. Every success generated more rigorous demands. You may be sure that there was no work stoppage under Pharaoh, because the production apparatus was at work 24/7. The production schedule, propelled by the king with the bad dreams, assumes that production that will enhance centralized authority is the purpose of all labor.

2. The aggressive policies of Pharaoh have a purpose other than mere exploitation. The narrative shows that Pharaoh is scared to death of his own workforce. He fears their departure, the loss of labor, and the humiliation of the empire. In his fear Pharaoh becomes even more abrasive, resolving to drive them crazy with exploitative work expectations:

> The Egyptians became ruthless in imposing tasks on the Israelites, and made their lives bitter with hard service in mortar and brick and in every kind of field labor. They were ruthless in all the tasks that they imposed on them. (Exod. 1:13–14)

The resounding word "ruthless" bespeaks an exploitative system that no longer thinks well about productivity. The fear that lies behind such policy finally leads to an assault on the labor force that provides for the killing of all baby boys that are potentially part of the workforce:

When you act as midwives to the Hebrew women, and see them on the birthstool, if it is a boy, kill him; but if it is a girl, she shall live. (v. 16)

The insanity of the policy is that Pharaoh now destroys precisely those who would be the next generation of workers. The narrative does not comment on the irony here, as in Genesis 41, that the one *with the most* is the one who is *most anxious* in irrational ways. His anxiety in Genesis 41 is unrelated to the reality of his food supply. And his anxiety here leads to self-destructive policies that contradict his own stated needs. Without calling attention to it, the narrative shows the way in which unrestrained power becomes destructive, both for those subject to that power and, eventually, for those who exercise such power as well.

3. The move from economic exploitation to policies that are grounded in fear seems deliberately designed to produce suffering. Finally, as every exploitative system eventually learns, the exploitation rooted in fear reaches its limit of unbearable suffering. Two things happen·

First, the unbearable suffering comes to public speech. Totalitarian regimes seek to keep suffering silent and invisible for as long as possible. And in this narrative, the silent slaves did not find their voice until Pharaoh died, the one who had been ruthless toward them. But of course, after Pharaoh dies, there will be another pharaoh, because there is always another pharaoh. In the face of this new pharaoh (who is, of course, unnamed), they find voice. They become agents in their own history, paying attention to their bodily pain and finding voice to match their pain. As every totalitarian regime eventually learns, human suffering will not stay silent. There is a cry! The irreducible human reality of suffering must finally have voice. It is only a cry, an articulation of raw bodily dismay. That is as close as we come in this narrative to prayer. Prayer here is truth—the truth of bodily pain—sounding its inchoate demand. The cry is not addressed to anyone. It is simply out there, declaring publicly that the social system of the empire has failed.

But second, as the biblical narrative has it—most remarkably—the cry of abused labor finds its way to the ears of YHWH, who, in this narrative, is reckoned to be a central player in the public drama of social power. The cry is not addressed to YHWH; but it comes to YHWH because YHWH is a magnet that draws the cries of the abused:[2]

Out of the slavery their cry for help rose up to God. God heard their groaning, and God remembered his covenant with Abraham, Isaac, and Jacob. God looked upon the Israelites, and God took notice of them. (Exod. 2:23b–25)

The human cry, so the Bible asserts, evokes divine resolve. There is a divine resolve to transform the economic situation of the slaves. It is, at the same time, inescapably, a divine resolve to delegitimate Pharaoh and to wrest social initiative away from the empire. YHWH makes no appearance in the early chapters of Exodus until it is time to respond to the cry of the slaves. It is the voice of the slaves, newly sounded, that draws YHWH actively into the narrative.

4. The practice of exploitation, fear, and suffering produces a decisive moment in human history. This dramatic turn away from aggressive centralized power and a food monopoly features a fresh divine resolve for an alternative possibility, a resolve that in turn features raw human agency. The biblical narrative is very careful and precise about how it transposes *divine resolve* into *human agency*. That transposition is declared in the encounter of the burning bush wherein Moses is addressed and summoned by this self-declaring God. The outcome of that inscrutable mystery of encounter is that Moses is invested with the vision of the slave community in its departure from the imperial economy. The words that go with the encounter are words of *divine resolve*:

Then the LORD said, "I have observed the misery of my people who are in Egypt; I have heard their cry on account of their taskmasters. Indeed, I know their sufferings, and I have come down to deliver them from the Egyptians, and to bring them up out of that land to a good and broad land, a land flowing with milk and honey, to the country of the Canaanites, the Hittites, the Amorites, the Perizzites, the Hivites, and the Jebusites. The cry of the Israelites has now come to me; I have also seen how the Egyptians oppress them." (Exod. 3:7–9)

But the divine resolve turns abruptly to human agency:

So come, I will send you to Pharaoh to bring my people, the Israelites, out of Egypt. (v. 10)

The outcome is a human agent who can act and dream outside imperial reality. And dreaming outside imperial reality, that human agent can begin the daring extrication of this people from the imperial system. Moses' childhood is unreported after his terror-laden birth story. Whatever may have been his Egyptian rootage (about which we know nothing), that rootage is not defining for the adult character of Moses in this narrative. His first adult appearance occurs when he goes out to "his people" and observes "their forced labor" (2:11). The pronouns are important. From the outset Moses is identified with the slave-labor force; his identity and his commitment are not in doubt. He lives in the context of forced labor. He sees a "brother" being abused by an Egyptian, an agent of Pharaoh's exploitative policies. No doubt the beating of the slave by the Egyptian was because the slave was not working hard enough or was recalcitrant against imperial authority. In any case, Moses—either as a freedom fighter for his people or as a terrorist against established authority, or both—kills the Egyptian agent of Pharaoh. Moses is ready to intervene against the empire on behalf of the exploited. Having struck a blow against the empire, Moses is a fugitive. Pharaoh, it is reported, "sought to kill" him (2:15). Moses from now on is completely resistant to the power of Pharaoh.

There is, surely, some high irony in the juxtaposition of Pharaoh and Moses. Pharaoh is a dreamer, but he dreams only of the nightmare of scarcity. But contrast Moses, who, after the burning bush, can indeed say, "I have a dream."

> I have a dream of departure,
> I have a dream beyond brick quotas,
> I have a dream beyond the regime of exploitation and fear,
> I have a dream outside the zone of strategically designed
>   suffering.

The dream of Moses sharply contrasts with the nightmare of Pharaoh. It is that dream that propels the biblical narrative. Pharaoh and Moses, along with all of his people, had been contained in a system of anxiety. There was enough anxiety for everyone, but there was not and could not be a common good. The anxiety system of Pharaoh precluded the common good. The imperial arrangement made everyone into a master or a slave, a threat or an accomplice, a rival or a slave. For the sake of the common good, it was necessary to depart *the anxiety system* that produces *nightmares of scarcity.*

III

The next chapter will explore in some detail the events through which
Israel achieves this emancipatory departure, but the ultimate outcome
of this paradigmatic performance of biblical salvation is that the for-
merly silent slaves tore themselves away from Pharaoh's system, even
though they later recalled that his system assured a steady stream of
food (see Num. 11:4–6). In Exodus 14 the slaves watched the waters
open for them (Exod. 14:21–23). They went through the deep waters
of risk where Pharaoh and his enforcers could not follow. In Exodus
15 they came out on the other side and danced for the first time, their
emancipated bodies now free of brick quotas, unencumbered by the
requirements of Pharaoh. Thus Moses sang: "The LORD will reign
forever and ever" (15:18). And Miriam and the other emancipated
women sang and danced: "Sing to the LORD, for he has triumphed
gloriously; horse and rider he has thrown into the sea" (v. 21).

Thus the slaves departed the anxiety system. And by Exodus 16,
they are underway on the long trek to well-being. In chapter 16 they
take their first generative steps out into the wilderness—the wilderness is where one ends up if one departs the anxiety system of Pharaoh. They are on their way, beyond the waters, through the desert,
toward a new covenantal shaping of life at Sinai. The sequence of
the plot makes clear, and continues to make clear, that the possibility of emancipation for covenantal alternative requires a departure
(exodus!) from the way the world conventionally maps power. That
conventional mapping of power does not take into account the col-
lusion of holy resolve and human cry, a combination that Pharaoh
found, eventually, to be irresistible.

This is a narrative that we keep reperforming as we have the courage to do so. We are, for the most part, timid and inured in Pharaoh's
narrative. His system has such a grip on us that we stay fixed on the
endless quotas of exploitation, quotas of production and consumption. That fix is evident even in the disciples of Jesus. Mark reports
of them: "They did not understand about the loaves, but their hearts
were hardened" (Mark 6:52). The reference to hard hearts means
that the disciples thought like Pharaoh, who had the quintessential
hard heart. They, like Pharaoh, thought in terms of acquisitiveness,
anxiety, and self-security. The result is that they could not understand

about the abundant bread given by the God of emancipation. They are so caught in that old ideology of power that they missed so much of the truth of distributive grace that was enacted in the old manna narrative and that is reiterated in the gospel of Jesus. It is no wonder that the narrative is always reperformed yet again, in order that we may recognize that recurring bondage among us and entertain that the departure from that bondage of one-dimensional power in response to the emancipatory truth is triggered by the cries of the oppressed.

Questions for Reflection

1. Brueggemann describes "the common good" as humanity's common destiny. This common destiny is disrupted by the "pharaohs" of our world, looking to hoard, create anxious systems, and center power. How would you describe, in contrast, "the common good"? Who are the pharaohs of our time disrupting our collective human destiny?

2. Pharaohs have motives, fears, anxieties. Their anxious dreams reflect vulnerable spaces that express the very things that could bring their demise. Think about the pharaohs of our time. What are their fears? How are they creating systems of anxiety and scarcity? Name some of the policies created through these nightmares.

3. As nightmarish policies become realistic and consequential, the people whose lives are burdened and whose bodies are marred cannot take it anymore. Their cries grow louder and louder. Where do you hear these cries? Who is shouting and crying out in your own community?

4. These cries are foundationally and fervently heard by the ever-present God who sides with the ones who are chained by oppression. And it is that God who calls to us through those burning-bush moments, inviting us to be human agents of a new reality. How are you dreaming of a new reality outside imperial reality? In what ways are you freeing yourself from systems of exploitation, productivity, and constant consumption?

Chapter 2

Plagues and Manna

Salvation through Divine Power
and Abundant Generosity

*T*he narrative of Israel's departure from the anxiety system of Pharaoh's Egypt is dramatic because it is fraught with contestations. Israel's geographic departure from Egyptian territory is resisted by royal powers that are reluctant to relinquish their labor supply or even to recognize an alternative ordering of social life. Yet this departure is also internally contested as Israel, following their physical exit from Egyptian territory, remains psychologically tempted to return to Egypt in the face of the risky abyss of emancipated life in the wilderness. Although the narrative foreshadows this second, existential obstacle to Israel's departure (e.g., in Exod. 6:9), the first and formidable obstacle to their departure and thus emancipation is Pharaoh's power, which is contested through the extended drama of the plagues (Exod. 7–11). The plagues are acts of disruptive, transformative power on the part of YHWH that serve to overwhelm the power and authority of Pharaoh and, consequently, to rescue the slaves from the power and authority of Pharaoh. The plagues are occasions of immense, inscrutable power that are taken to be signs of YHWH's sovereignty, not at all to be explained naturalistically, as has been frequently attempted. They are not to be understood naturalistically because they make immediate and direct appeal to the hidden, odd power of YHWH, without which they have no force in the narrative. They are exhibits of awesome divine power and resolve before which the anxious power of Pharaoh proves helpless.

I

The immediate effect of the plagues is in order that "the Egyptians may know that I am YHWH" (7:5, auth. trans.). The verb "know" is used in a double sense of (a) having convincing data, but also (b) acknowledging as sovereign. The slow sequence of plagues evidences that Pharaoh, little by little, began to acknowledge and concede, in grudging ways, the rule of YHWH, so that Pharaoh must eventually confess his sin and ask forgiveness (10:16–17). In the end, Pharaoh even acknowledges that the power to bless resides among the Israelites (12:32). The consequence of such a show of power is that Israel also may "know that I am YHWH," that is, recognize YHWH's real sovereignty over Pharaoh's pseudo-sovereignty, and so receive the gift of freedom given by YHWH (10:1–2). Thus the plague narrative constitutes disclosure (both to Egypt the oppressor and to the oppressed slaves) of the way YHWH presides over power relations in history, YHWH's governance is to the astonishing benefit of the slaves. The narrative account has no reservation in exhibiting YHWH's capacity to manage the wonders of creation in order to evoke historical newness (Israel) as an outcome of disordering and reordering creation.[1]

After the river is turned to blood (7:14–25) and after the frogs (8:1–15), the third round of the contest concerns gnats. After the two rounds of contested power that ended in a draw, in the third try the Egyptian technicians (the roster of learned men in and of the empire) could not match the power of YHWH: "They could not!" (8:18). They are not able! The power of Pharaoh has reached its limit in a dramatic way. Pharaonic power does not run as far as YHWH's power enacted by Moses and Aaron. (The failure on gnats is like not having an atomic bomb, thus a poor competitor in the big race.) After that, it is a mop-up action for YHWH, with Pharaoh making a reluctant, grudging retreat before the saving power of YHWH-cum-Moses.

By Exodus 8:25, Pharaoh knows that he must compromise, because his power is not absolute any longer. He is prepared to let the slaves "sacrifice to your God," but "within the land," that is, under supervision and surveillance. When Moses refuses that grudging offer, Pharaoh grants a permit to go into the wilderness, but "do not go very far away" (v. 28). And then, Pharaoh petitions Moses,

"Pray for me" (v. 28). The narrative permits Pharaoh a slight dawning about the new, changed world he must now inhabit in which he must yield small bits of power. His conduct is the usual way of an overthrown dictator who always catches on slowly about the new flow of power and who always makes small concessions without recognizing that the game is in fact over.

By 10:8, Pharaoh concedes that some may leave to worship YHWH, that is, to change loyalties, but then he asks as a ploy, "But which ones are to go?" It is as though the tyrant allows a quota to depart and then requires the leader to select who will go and who must remain. And we know, from the death camps in Germany, about selection. Of course Moses refuses and declares that none will go until all go—an anticipation of the way in which Nelson Mandela refused the chance to depart prison early without his companions.

By 10:24, Pharaoh wants to hold only the flocks and herds of Israel as surety:

> Go, worship the LORD. Only your flocks and your herds shall remain behind. Even your children may go with you. (v. 24)

Moses again refuses: "Not a hoof shall be left behind" (v. 26). Moses knows that the tide has turned, and he has no need to compromise with Pharaoh.

Pharaoh twice concedes that he has sinned:

> This time I have sinned; the LORD is in the right, and I and my people are in the wrong. Pray to the LORD. Enough of God's thunder and hail! I will let you go; you need stay no longer. (9:27–28)

> I have sinned against the LORD your God, and against you. Do forgive my sin just this once, and pray to the LORD your God that at the least he remove this deadly thing from me. (10:16–17)

Pharaoh now knows! But he cannot bring himself to face the fact that the truth of the slaves-cum-YHWH has undone his shaky claim to power and has negated whatever legitimacy he may have once had. The confession and the prayer of Pharaoh constitute an acknowledgment of YHWH, but Moses takes them to be strategic ploys rather than authentic recognition. And so Moses responds yet again:

> As soon as I have gone out of the city, I will stretch out my hands
> to the LORD; the thunder will cease, and there will be no more hail,
> so that you may know that the earth is the LORD's. (9:29)

Pharaoh must know fully, must acknowledge, must concede, must yield.
And indeed, by 10:7 Pharaoh is the only one left who will not
yield. His most trusted advisers know better:

> Pharaoh's officials said to him, "How long shall this fellow be a
> snare to us? Let the people go, so that they may worship the LORD
> their God; do you not yet understand that Egypt is ruined?"

This counsel to the king is not unlike the way in which the advisers
to Lyndon Johnson all knew that the war in Vietnam was lost and
now could only destroy what was left of Johnson's political legacy.
So it was with Pharaoh. His policy of resistance left Pharaoh and his
regime in shambles. But such raw power that imagines itself to be
absolute never learns in time.

In the concluding scene of this drama, Pharaoh, now of necessity
alert to the emancipatory truth of YHWH, summons Moses and says
to him:

> Rise up, go away from my people, both you and the Israelites! Go,
> worship the LORD, as you said. Take your flocks and your herds,
> as you said, and be gone. (12:31–32)

Power must now acknowledge *truth*. The truth that meets power here
is the combination of attentive *divine resolve* and the *bodily assertion* of the slaves who suffer out loud. Pharaoh, the last to catch on,
now knows that his exploitative power has no future. Indeed, by the
end he knows even more than that; he knows about "the migration
of the holy."[2] God's holiness has departed Egypt and has settled on
this company of shrill, demanding, enraged slaves. And so he says
in his last utterance in this dramatic narrative: "And bring a blessing
on me too!" (v. 32).

In this utterance we have the great Egyptian embodiment of
worldly power on its knees, in supplication, asking that the power for
life from God, that is "blessing," be given by this fugitive who car-
ries radical public truth that is effective transformative power. This
climactic utterance is breathtaking in its recognition that the locus

of power has shifted; holiness is allied with unbearable human pain now brought to speech and to active power.[3]

As you know, the text is not reportage; it is, rather, critical reflection based on memory at some distance from what may have happened. The narrators characterize this self-conscious interpretive intentionality in 10:1–2. Pharaoh operated with a hard heart, that is, he conceded and retracted and conceded and retracted, in order, they say, to keep the story going episode after episode:

> in order that I may show these signs of mine among them, and that you may tell your children and grandchildren how I made fools of the Egyptians and what signs I have done among them—so that you may know that I am the LORD.

The purpose is to attest the power of YHWH as player in the public drama. More than that, the purpose is to tell the grandchildren. This is a teaching curriculum in a narrative form so that you and your grandchildren, unlike Pharaoh, will learn to know YHWH in time. The intent is that you will recognize that the map of power and truth is complex and multidimensional. The story is reiterated in order that the coming generation should not be seduced by Pharaoh's simplistic reading of power that is impervious to the transformative potential of social pain when it is enacted in the public domain.

II

After departing the anxiety system of Pharaoh's Egypt, the slaves enter a very different sort of narrative in the wilderness, where it becomes clear that biblical salvation involves more than physical departure. Such departure is essential, difficult, and risky, but it does not realize true emancipation for the characters in the biblical drama. The wilderness is a place where numerous inexplicable and unreal miracles occur, but the biblical story is deeply realistic in its refusal to portray salvation as an easy, miraculous event that immediately embraces those who leave Egypt behind. The wilderness provides a training ground for Israel to begin to inhabit an alternative, emancipated, and flourishing communal life.

Yet Egypt proves difficult for them to leave behind, even as the narrative continues to develop toward the realization of their salvation through a series of events culminating in the new instructions that they receive at Sinai for a covenantal shaping of their lives. By verse 3 of Exodus 16, deep in the wilderness, they began to complain about their new environment of risky faith; they yearned to resubmit to the anxious exploitation of Pharaoh:

> The Israelites said to them, "If only we had died by the hand of the LORD in the land of Egypt, when we sat by the fleshpots and ate our fill of bread; for you have brought us out into this wilderness to kill this whole assembly with hunger." (Exod. 16:3)

They remembered slavery as a place of guaranteed food. Later they would recall their slave diet with some relish:

> The rabble among them had a strong craving; and the Israelites also wept again, and said, "If only we had meat to eat! We remember the fish we used to eat in Egypt for nothing, the cucumbers, the melons, the leeks, the onions, and the garlic; but now our strength is dried up, and there is nothing at all but this manna to look at." (Num. 11:4–6)

Their endless complaint mobilized Moses, who in turn complained to God, and God responded to the complaint; perhaps the divine response was a necessity because now YHWH, and not Pharaoh, is responsible for this people. YHWH issues an assurance:

> I have heard the complaining of the Israelites; say to them, "At twilight you shall eat meat, and in the morning you shall have your fill of bread; then you shall know that I am the LORD your God." (Exod. 16:12)

The meat will be quail and that came as promised. And concerning bread in the morning the narrative reports:

> When the layer of dew lifted, there on the surface of the wilderness was a fine flaky substance, as fine as frost on the ground. (v. 14)

The "bread of heaven" was like nothing they knew, and so they said to one another, as they watched the gift of bread fall on them, "What is it?" The Hebrew for that question is *man hu'*, and so the bread is called "manna." The bread is named "What is it?" which makes it a "wonder bread" that fit none of their prevailing categories; they wondered what it was.

Now it takes little imagination to see that this narrative of bread in the wilderness is a very different sort of narrative contrasted with that of the exodus. The exodus narrative is credible and realistic, all about exploited cheap labor and escape from an impossible production schedule. Compared with that, this narrative of bread from heaven is a dreamy narrative that lacks that kind of realism. But then, consider that there is something inescapably dreamy and unreal about inexplicable generosity. When we hear of it we wonder about it and doubt it, because it does not fit our expectations for a quid pro quo world. Indeed, about such divine generosity there is something so dreamy that we reserve for it the special term *miracle*, something outside the ordinary, something that breaks the pattern of the regular and the expected, something that violates the predictable. So consider this sequence of great words, "dreamy, inexplicable, generous, miracle."

Finally we will come to the word *grace*, a reach of divine generosity not based on the recipient but on the giver. If we juxtapose the words *grace* and *wilderness*, we come to the claim of this narrative of wonder bread. "Wilderness" is a place, in biblical rhetoric, where there are no viable life-support systems. "Grace" is the occupying generosity of God that redefines the place. The wonder bread, as a gesture of divine grace, recharacterizes the wilderness that Israel now discovered to be a place of viable life, made viable by the generous inclination of YHWH.

If we pursue this juxtaposition of "grace" and "wilderness," later we will find it explicit in the poetry of the prophet Jeremiah. That prophet uses the word *wilderness* to refer to the sixth-century exile, a subsequent locus for the life of Israel that also lacked viable life supports. In that locus of death, Israel found sustaining divine presence, so that the prophet can say of God's miracle:

> Thus says the LORD:
> The people who survived the sword
>   found *grace* in the *wilderness*;
> when Israel sought for rest,
>   the LORD appeared to him from far away.
>   Jer. 31:2–3a

It is impossible to overstate the significance of "grace in the wilderness," given in the palpable form of bread that could sustain in an unsustainable context. That moment of wonder, awe, and generosity, in an instant, radically redefined the place in which Israel now had to live in its new freedom, outside the zone of imperial anxiety.

So, the narrative tells us, the bread in the wilderness was a divine gesture of enormous abundance:

> Moses said to them, "It is the bread that the LORD has given you to eat. This is what the LORD has commanded: 'Gather as much of it as each of you needs, an omer to a person according to the number of persons, all providing for those in their own tents.'" The Israelites did so, some gathering more, some less. But when they measured it with an omer, those who gathered much had nothing over, and those who gathered little had no shortage; they gathered as much as each of them needed. (Exod. 16:15–18)

This narrative stands at the center of Israel's imagination; it embodies and signifies YHWH's *capacity for generosity* that stands in complete contrast to the *nightmare of scarcity* that fueled Pharaoh's rapacious policies. The Israelites were so inured to the scarcity system of Pharaoh that they could hardly take in the alternative abundance given in divine generosity, the purpose of which was to break the vicious cycle of anxiety about scarcity that in turn produced anger, fear, aggression, and, finally, predatory violence.

The Israelites, in the narrative, are overwhelmed by divine abundance. They react, however, as though they were still in the old system of pharaonic scarcity. Moses warned them not to save up or to hoard the bread or to keep extra supplies on hand:

> And Moses said to them, "Let no one leave any of it over until morning." (v. 19)

Take what you need, eat and enjoy! But they did not listen. They filled their pockets and their baskets with extras because there might not be any more tomorrow. That is what one does in the face of scarcity. (In Atlanta, where we never have snow, a rumor of a snowflake will cause grocery shelves to rapidly become empty, storing up for another day when things might be scarce.)

But such frantic surpluses will not work. Because the "bread of heaven" is not like the "bread of affliction" that the Israelites had eaten in Egyptian slavery. There you could save a crust of bread for the next day. But not here! Abundance is not for hoarding. So, we are told:

> They did not listen to Moses; some left part of it until morning, and it *bred worms* and *became foul*. And Moses was angry with them. Morning by morning they gathered it, as much as each needed; but when the sun grew hot, it *melted*. (vv. 20–21)

The stored-up bread *bred worms*. It *smelled bad*. It *melted*. It would not last. Wonder bread lacks preservatives, because it is given daily, enough but not more, enough so that none need hunger. The bread of heaven is a contradiction to the rat race of production; the creator God who presides over the bread supply breaks the grip of Pharaoh's food monopoly; food is freely given outside the economic system that functions like an Egyptian pyramid with only a few on top of the heap.[4]

III

It is for good reason that in the Bible "bread" is the recurring sign of divine generosity, because it is the concrete indispensable resource for life in the world. In the narrative of the prophet Elisha, among the wonder men in ancient Israel, the narratives are often about bread:

- In 2 Kings 4:1–7 there is the abundant gift of oil given by the prophet so the widow can pay her debts and prepare bread for the future.
- In 2 Kings 4:42–44 the same prophet has a limited supply of bread. But he feeds one hundred people and "has some left." The narrative attests that where the carriers of God's truth are at work, abundance overrides the scarcity of hunger.
- In 2 Kings 6:22–23, in the midst of Israel's perpetual war with Syria, the same prophet intervenes. The king of Israel wants to kill his Syrian prisoners of war, but the prophet will not permit it. Instead of death to the enemies, the prophet commands:

> Set food and water before them so that they may eat and drink; and let them go to their master. (v. 22)

And the outcome of the generous meal:

> So he prepared for them a great feast; after they ate and drank,
> he sent them on their way, and they went to their master. And the
> Arameans no longer came raiding into the land of Israel. (v. 23)

A "great feast" breaks the pattern of violence that is rooted in a fear
of scarcity. The narrative attests that the world is not as we had imagined it, not as Pharaoh had organized it. Adherence to patterns of
scarcity produces a world in which the generosity of God is nullified.
The narratives attest otherwise and invite the listening community
into an alternative mode of existence, one that is ordered according
to divine generosity.

It is not different later in the poetry of Isaiah. In Isaiah 55 it is
clear that the displaced Jews had fallen into the trap of the imperial
system of Babylon. They had been carried away into the empire. For
Jews with a long memory, being carried to Babylon was like being
taken back to Pharaoh's Egypt, because all empires act the same way.
All empires act according to the principle of scarcity, imagining that
they need more land, more tax money, more revenue, more oil, more
cheap labor, more energy. Some Jews had signed on for the new
scarcity system that was just like the old scarcity system, once again
inured to imperial expectation that left them frazzled, exhausted, and
cynical, because empires set quotas that can never be met.

In the midst of that new, unbearable context of scarcity, a context shaped not by facts on the ground but by ideological force, the
prophet interrupts with an assertion and a question that raises hard
issues about imperial ideology:

> Ho, everyone who thirsts,
>   come to the waters;
> and you that have no money,
>   come, buy and eat!
> Come, buy wine and milk
>   without money and without price.
>   Isa. 55:1

Free food, free water, free milk, free wine—more than enough. The
old divine gift of abundance in the wilderness is now renewed as
abundance in exile. Then the question, which in fact is an accusation:

Why do you spend your money for that which is not bread,
   and your labor for that which does not satisfy?
Listen carefully to me, and eat what is good,
   and delight yourselves in rich food.

v. 2

The question is to Israelites, people of faith, who have succumbed
to the scarcity system of Babylon, who have joined the rat race, and
who have imagined that they could get ahead if they hustled more.
The poet asks why they do that: "Why do you sign on for scarcity
when you know the truth of God's abundance?"

Then comes a summons that follows from the *assurance of generosity* and the *question about the present scarcity*:

Seek the LORD while he may be found,
   call upon him while he is near;
let the wicked forsake their way,
   and the unrighteous their thoughts;
let them return to the LORD, that he may have mercy on them,
   and to our God, for he will abundantly pardon.

vv. 6–7

In specific location, this text is not a generic concern for sin and
salvation. It is, rather, a summons away from the *scarcity system* to
the *truth of generosity*. In location the text is a summons to be a Jew
with memories of abundance and a call to disengage from the ideology of scarcity that propels the empire. The poet knows that unless
this summons is heeded, his listeners will remain perpetually unsatisfied, because the imperial pursuit of "more" can never be satisfied.
Pharaoh can never have enough to sleep well at night. Pharaoh's
ideology of anxiety will impinge upon sleep even as it defines the
economy. Both sleep and the economy remain restless!

What Israel discovered in the wilderness—and again in the
exile—is that there is an alternative. Indeed, it is fair to say that the
long history of Israel is a contestation between *Pharaoh's system
of paucity* and *God's offer of abundance*. Surely it is a legitimate
extrapolation that the long history of the church is a contest between
paucity that presses to control and *abundance* that evokes patterns of
generosity. Beyond Israel or church, going all the way back to Erik
Erikson's elemental "basic trust," the human enterprise is a contrast

between scarcity and the dreaminess of abundance that breaks the compulsions of scarcity.[5] Israel, full of wonder bread, makes its way to Mount Sinai. That gift of wonder *bread* as a miracle of *abundance* is a show of *generosity* that breaks the deathly pattern of anxiety, fear, greed, and anger, a *miracle* that always surprises because it is beyond our categories of expectation. It is precisely an overwhelming, inexplicable act of generosity that breaks the grip of self-destructive anxiety concerning scarcity.

IV

So they came to Sinai. They came from the *nightmare of paucity* by way of the *miracle of abundance*. What they discovered, as they approached the dread mountain of covenant, is that the gift of shalom had freed them from pharaonic scarcity so that they could have energy for the common good. They discovered at Mount Sinai that they could give energy to the neighborhood because the grip of *scarcity* had been broken by God's *abundance*. As they approached the mountain, long before they had heard any of God's commandments, they asserted, already in Exodus 19:8,

> The people all answered as one: "Everything that the LORD has spoken we will do."

Israel signed on for a new obedience even before they had heard any of the commandments! The reason they did so is that they knew that any new commands from the God of abundance would be better than the commands of Pharaoh. The new commands at Sinai voiced YHWH's dream of a neighborhood, YHWH's intention for the common good. There was no common good in Egypt, because people in a scarcity system cannot entertain the common good.

This narrative from *anxiety* through *abundance* to *neighborhood* invites us to rethink the intention of the Ten Commandments, to which we will turn our attention in the next section. They are not rules for deep moralism. They are not commonsense rules designed to clobber and scold people. Rather, they are the most elemental statement of how to organize social power and social goods for the common benefit of the community. They are indeed "a new commandment" that is quite in contrast to the old commandments of Pharaoh.

Questions for Reflection

1. Central to the exodus story are the plagues, which display the divine power of YHWH and pressure Pharaoh into concession. In our current world, have you experienced this type of divine power, which disorders in order to reorder creation? Recount a moment in your life when you have been confronted with disorder and chaos. How did this "plague" reorient you, and how did it change your view of power?

2. As Pharaoh comes to the realization that the power of YHWH would overcome the power of imperial rule, YHWH weaves into the tapestry of faith the importance of teaching the next generations of Israelites this new narrative about power. What are you teaching the next generations about the power of God versus the power of empire? How are you helping to pass down the dream of abundance and abolish the nightmare of scarcity?

3. The wilderness is a literal and metaphorical setting in which the Israelites wonder, complain, and yearn for the imperial system of Egypt they are already familiar with. And yet, the wilderness also becomes a place where grace permeates lifelessness and creates life. Reflect on a time in your life when you were in a space of "wilderness." Where did you experience divine grace? At what moment did you receive manna or "the wonder bread"?

4. The manna from YHWH is a gift given out of abundance, the generous energy that breaks the cycles of cultures of scarcity. As you continue to creatively engage the reality of this abundance, how do you imagine growing communities that are rooted in following a God of miracles beyond our expectation? What does that look like for you?

PART TWO

Initial Instructions at Sinai: The Ten Commandments

Chapter 3

The First Commandments

Choosing One's God

*O*ur consideration of salvation in the Bible rightly begins with the story of the exodus. And yet, as we have already seen, emancipation in the Bible involves more than an exit from Egypt. Indeed, all roads out of Egypt lead to Sinai. The Israelites had escaped Egyptian slavery, though they remembered Pharaoh's Egypt wistfully as a place of adequate food. They had traversed the "stony road" of wilderness, been contentious, and received "wonder bread" from the sky. Then they approached the mountain. It was an awesome, dread-filled place that signaled divine presence that was in no sense user-friendly. As they approached that dread mountain, Moses reminded them of the heavy cost of life with YHWH. They would have to obey:

> Now therefore, if you obey my voice and keep my covenant, you shall be my treasured possession out of all the peoples. Indeed, the whole earth is mine, but you shall be for me a priestly kingdom and a holy nation. These are the words that you shall speak to the Israelites. (Exod. 19:5–6)

The mountain was an offer of a new identity, of life in covenant with YHWH. That is all Moses said. He gave them no detail. But Israel, in its eagerness, answered quickly and without reservation:

> The people all answered as one: "Everything that the LORD has spoken we will do." Moses reported the words of the people to the LORD. (v. 8)

They answered with promptness and eagerness, even though they did not know the particulars. I imagine, would you not, that the reason

31

for their ready affirmation is that they knew that whatever YHWH required would be less than Pharaoh required. They were prepared to try the new "boss," who would surely be better than the exploitative brutality of the old boss.

So they approached the mountain. As they approached, the mountain shook and trembled with smoke and fire. The mountain surged and shrieked with divine presence. This is the hidden, inscrutable, savage God who inhabits the mountain and who, like a fairy-tale ogre, threatens all who approach.

And then the God of the mountain spoke. This was a strange God, whom they did not know. First, this God tells his name. This name, however we are to take it, is a set of consonants with ill-fitting vowels. Christian scholars say "YHWH"; Jews refuse to say it. The name is an enigma, except the utterance fills out the inscrutable name, ". . . who brought you out of the land of Egypt, out of the house of bondage." Surprise! The God they had already known as their great advocate and emancipator turns out to be the God of the mountain. This is the God who, on their behalf, outmatched and outmuscled Pharaoh, terminated the brick quota, and ended the hot, demanding brickyards. That is the God who speaks, who now offers a charter for an alternative existence outside the categories of Pharaoh.

As you know, this mountain God of freedom speaks ten times, only ten, and then not again at Sinai, for after that everything comes via Moses. These ten utterances constitute the only direct speech of YHWH. As he spoke ten times, he spoke three times about the *love of God*, "love" being a covenant word for honoring treaty commitments. You know them, no rival gods, no manufactured replicas as fetishes, and no words that reduce God to a means. A pause, and then he spoke six times about *love of neighbor*, "love" being a covenant word for honoring treaty commitments. You know these six about parents and killing and committing adultery and stealing and giving false witness and coveting. Three for God and six for neighbor—nine altogether, love of God and love of neighbor, the two great commands. And then this emancipatory voice circled back and pressed the "insert" button on his computer; YHWH inserted between the three on *love of God* and six on *love of neighbor*, the longest of all commands, the commandment on Sabbath.

Patrick Miller has shrewdly observed that the fourth commandment, on Sabbath, is the "crucial bridge" that connects the Ten Commandments together.[1] The fourth commandment looks back to the first three commandments and the God of restfulness (Exod. 20:3–7). At the same time, the Sabbath commandment looks forward to the last six commandments that concern the neighbor who needs restfulness (vv. 12–17). The commands about Sabbath thus provide for rest alongside the neighbor. God, self, and all members of the household share in common rest on the seventh day; that social reality provides a commonality and a coherence not only to the community of covenant but to the commandments of Sinai as well. For that reason, it is appropriate in our study of biblical salvation that we include several reflections on these commandments, beginning here and continuing in subsequent chapters.

I

The first commandments concern God, God's aniconic character, and God's name (vv. 3–7). But when we consider the identity of this God, we are made immediately aware that the God who will brook no rival and who eventually will rest is a God who is embedded in a narrative; this God is not known or available apart from that narrative. The narrative matrix of YHWH, the God of Israel, is the exodus narrative. This is the God "who brought you out of the land of Egypt, out of the house of slavery" (v. 2). Thus the commandments are drawn into the exodus narrative, for the God who rests is the God who emancipates *from slavery* and consequently *from the work system of Egypt* and *from the gods of Egypt* who require and legitimate that work system. It is, for that reason, fair to judge that the prohibition against "the other gods" in the first commandment pertains directly to the gods of Egypt (see Exod. 12:12) and other gods of the same ilk in Canaan, or subsequently the gods of the great empires of Assyria, Babylon, or Persia. In the narrative imagination of Israel, the gods of Egypt are stand-ins for all the gods of the empires. What they all have in common is that they are confiscatory gods who demand endless produce and who authorize endless systems of production that are, in principle, insatiable. Thus, the mention of "Egypt" brings the God of Israel into the orbit of socioeconomic systems and practices, and inevitably sets this God on a collision course with the gods of insatiable productivity.

The reference to "Egypt" indicates that the God of Sinai who gives the Ten Commandments is never simply a "religious figure" but is always preoccupied with and attentive to socioeconomic practice and policy. If we want, then, to understand this God (or any god), we must look to the socioeconomic system that that god legitimates and authorizes. In the case of the Egyptian gods (who are in contrast to and in competition with the God of the exodus), we look to Pharaoh's system of production that is legitimated by the gods worshiped by Pharaoh. In Exodus 5, we are given a passionate narrative account of that labor system, in which Pharaoh endlessly demands more production. What the slaves are to produce is more bricks that are to be used for the building of more "supply cities" in which Pharaoh can store his endless supply of material wealth in the form of grain (see Exod. 1:11). Because the system was designed to produce more and more surplus (see Gen. 47:13–26), there is always more need for storage units that in turn generated more need for bricks with which to construct them. Thus, if we follow the required bricks from the slave camps, we end with surplus wealth, taken as a gift of the gods of Pharaoh. In this narrative report, Pharaoh is a hard-nosed production manager for whom production schedules are inexhaustible:

- "[W]hy are you taking the people away from their work? Get to your labors!" (Exod. 5:4)
- ". . . . yet you want them to stop working!" (v. 5)
- "You shall no longer give the people straw to make bricks, as before; let them go and gather straw for themselves. But you shall require of them the same quantity of bricks as they have made previously; do not diminish it, for they are lazy." (vv. 7–8)
- "Let heavier work be laid on them; then they will labor at it and pay no attention to deceptive words." (v. 9)
- "I will not give you straw. Go and get straw yourselves, wherever you can find it; but your work will not be lessened in the least." (vv. 10–11)

- "Complete your work, the same daily assignment as when you were given straw." (v. 13)
- "Why did you not finish the required quantity of bricks yesterday and today, as you did before?" (v. 14)
- "No straw is given to your servants, yet they say to us, 'Make bricks.'" (v. 16)
- "You are lazy, lazy; that is why you say, 'Let us go and sacrifice to the LORD.' Go now, and work; for no straw shall be given you, but you shall still deliver the same number of bricks." (vv. 17–18)
- "You shall not lessen your daily number of bricks." (v. 19)

The rhetoric is relentless, all to the single point, as relentless as is the production schedule.

It is clear that in this system there can be no Sabbath rest. There is no rest for Pharaoh in his supervisory capacity, and he undoubtedly monitors daily production schedules. Consequently, there can be no rest for Pharaoh's supervisors or taskmasters; and of course there can be no rest for the slaves, who must satisfy the taskmasters in order to meet Pharaoh's demanding quotas. We may imagine, moreover, that the "Egyptian gods" also never rested, because of their commitment to the aggrandizement of Pharaoh's system, for the glory of Pharaoh surely redounded to the glory of the Egyptian gods. The economy reflects the splendor of the gods who legitimate the entire system, for which cheap labor is an indispensable footnote!

It requires no imagination to see that the exodus memory and consequently the Sinai commandments are performed in a "no Sabbath" environment. In that context, all levels of social power—gods, Pharaoh, supervisors, taskmasters, slaves—are uniformly caught up in and committed to the grind of endless production.

Into this system of hopeless weariness erupts the God of the burning bush (Exod. 3:1–6). That God heard the despairing fatigue of the slaves (2:23–25), resolved to liberate the slave company of Israel from that exploitative system (3:7–9), and recruited Moses for the human task of emancipation (3:10). The reason Miriam and the other women can sing and dance at the end of the exodus narrative is the emergence of a new social reality in which the life of the Israelite economy is no longer determined and compelled by the insatiable production quotas of Egypt and its gods (15:20–21).

The first commandment is a declaration that the God of the exodus is unlike all the gods the slaves have known heretofore. This God is not to be confused with or thought parallel to the insatiable gods of imperial productivity. This God is subsequently revealed as a God of mercy, steadfast love, and faithfulness, who is committed to covenantal relationships of fidelity (see 34:6–7). At the taproot of this divine commitment to *relationship* (*covenant*) rather than *commodity* (*bricks*) is the capacity and willingness of this God to rest. The Sabbath rest of God is the acknowledgment that God and God's people in the world are not commodities to be dispatched for endless production, as we used to say, as "hands" in the service of a command economy. Rather, they are subjects situated in an economy of neighborliness. All of that is implicit in the reality and exhibit of divine rest.

Thus the Sabbath command of Exodus 20:11 recalls that God rested on the seventh day of creation, an allusion to Genesis 2:1–4. That divine rest on the seventh day of creation has made clear (a) that YHWH is not a workaholic, (b) that YHWH is not anxious about the full functioning of creation, and (c) that the well-being of creation does not depend on endless work. This performance and exhibit of divine rest thus characterize the God of creation, creation itself, and the creatures made in the image of the resting God. Creation is to be enacted and embraced without defining anxiety. Indeed, such divine rest serves to delegitimate and dismantle the endless restlessness sanctioned by the other gods and enacted by their adherents. That divine rest on the seventh day, moreover, is recalled in the commandment of Exodus 31:12–17, wherein God is "refreshed" on the seventh day. The God of Israel (and of creation) is no immovable, fixed object, but here is said to be depleted and by rest may recover a full sense of "self " (*nephesh*).

II

The second commandment is closely related to the first. The commandment against "graven images" (idols) is a prohibition against any artistic representation of YHWH, for such representation would serve to "locate" YHWH, to domesticate God, and so to curb the freedom that belongs to this erupting God (Exod. 20:4–6; see 2 Sam. 7:6–7). Such images have the effect of drawing God, in imagination and in practice, away from covenantal, relational fidelity and back into a world of objects and commodities. The temptation to produce an "image" of God in artistic form is always, everywhere a chance to produce a commodity out of valuable material, at best gold if available, or lesser valuable material if not. When a god is fashioned into a golden commodity (or even lesser material), divine subject becomes divine object, and agent becomes commodity. We may cite two obvious examples of this temptation in the Old Testament. First, in the narrative of the "Golden Calf" in Exodus 32, it was gold that was fashioned into the image that readily became an alternative god who jeopardized the covenant. The ensuing narrative of Exodus 33–34 tells of the hard and tricky negotiations whereby covenantal possibility is restored to Israel after its foray into distorting images (Exod. 34:9–10). Less dramatically, it is evident that Solomon's temple, designed to "house" YHWH, became a commodity enterprise preoccupied with gold:

> The interior of the inner sanctuary was twenty cubits long, twenty cubits wide, and twenty cubits high; he overlaid it with pure *gold*. He also overlaid the altar with cedar. Solomon overlaid the inside of the house with pure *gold*, then he drew chains of *gold* across, in front of the inner sanctuary, and overlaid it with *gold*. Next he overlaid the whole house with *gold*, in order that the whole house might be perfect; even the whole altar that belonged to the inner sanctuary he overlaid with *gold*. (1 Kgs. 6:20–22, emphasis added)

> So Solomon made all the vessels that were in the house of the LORD: the *golden* altar, the *golden* table for the bread of the Presence, the lampstands of pure *gold*, five on the south side and five on the north, in front of the inner sanctuary; the flowers, the lamps, and the tongs, of *gold*; the cups, snuffers, basins, dishes for incense, and firepans, of pure *gold*; the sockets for the doors of the innermost part of the house, the most holy place, and for the doors of the nave of the temple, of *gold*. (7:48–50, emphasis added)

Even as YHWH was honored by such extravagance, the temple was clearly intended to reflect honor on Solomon and his regime. The attention to gold objects clearly skewed the simple and direct matter of covenantal possibility. Commodity desire has, for the most part, crowded out the covenantal tradition.

In the modern world, Karl Marx reflected most deeply on the compelling power of commodity. He took his famous phrase "commodity fetishism" from current study of the history of religions in which it was judged that "primitives" had such fetishes that occupied their desire and their devotion. Marx transferred that idea from "primitive" practice to modern market fascination and came to see that possessing commodities of social value generated a desire for more such value, so that commodity took on a power of its own that consisted of desire for more and more. It is easy enough to see Pharaoh's compulsion for more grain (a measure of wealth) beyond anything he could have needed, simply so that he could exhibit his great wealth and power. His desire for more created a restlessness that could permit no Sabbath rest for himself or any in his domain. And clearly Solomon is sketched out as the one who would possess all of his available world in his insatiable need for more (see 10:14–25).

For good reason the book of Deuteronomy ponders the force and danger of "images of God." In what is likely a late exposition of the first two commandments, this sermonic chapter looks back to the danger done by "commodity religion":

> Since you saw no form when the LORD spoke to you at Horeb out of the fire, take care and watch yourselves closely, so that you do not act corruptly by making an idol for yourselves, in the form of any figure—the likeness of male or female, the likeness of any animal that is on the earth, the likeness of any winged bird that flies in the air, the likeness of anything that creeps on the ground, the likeness of any fish that is in the water under the earth. And when you look up to the heavens and see the sun, the moon, and the stars, all the host of heaven, do not be led astray and bow down to them and serve them, things that the LORD your God has allotted to all the peoples everywhere under heaven. (Deut. 4:15–19)

The danger is to compromise the peculiarity of YHWH and of Israel.

After this inventory of possible images, the rhetoric of verse 20 voices the alternative:

But the LORD has taken you and brought you out of the iron-smelter, out of Egypt, to become a people of his very own possession, as you are now.

The emancipatory gift of YHWH to Israel is contrasted with all the seductions of images. The memory of the exodus concerns the God of freedom who frees. The clear implication is that fixed images preclude freedom and become icons of stable equilibrium. Such image-religion becomes a way of sustaining status-quo socioeconomic power that negates the emancipatory impulse of Israel's God and Israel's defining narrative. Thus it is credible to see that the culmination of *creation* in Sabbath and the culmination of *exodus* in Sabbath together refuse Pharaoh's pursuit of commodity. This refusal is decisive for Israel's faith and Israel's management of the economy: Do not worship such objects or make them your defining desire! That radical either-or is precisely the issue of the first commandment. It concerns the two temptations Israel faced, a temptation toward idols and an economic temptation of Israel to commodity.

YHWH is a Sabbath-keeping God, which ensures that restfulness and not restlessness is at the center of life. YHWH is a Sabbath-giving God and a Sabbath-commanding God. Israel, for that reason, is always again to re-choose between "life and death" (Deut. 30:15–20), between YHWH and "the gods of your ancestors" (Josh. 24:14–15), between YHWH and Baal (1 Kgs. 18:21), between the way of Torah and the way of sinners (Ps. 1). Sabbath becomes a decisive, concrete, visible way of opting for and aligning with the God of rest.

That same either-or is evident in the teaching of Jesus. In his Sermon on the Mount, he declares to his disciples:

No one can serve two masters; for a slave will either hate the one and love the other, or be devoted to the one and despise the other. You cannot serve God and wealth. (Matt. 6:24)

The way of *mammon* (capital, wealth) is the way of commodity, which is the way of endless desire, endless productivity, and endless restlessness without any Sabbath. Jesus taught his disciples that they could not have it both ways.

In the tradition of Matthew, the next verses (vv. 25–33) exposit the power of anxiety as the alternative to trust. It is, of course, in the same gospel tradition that Jesus comes to these familiar words:

> Come to me, all you that are weary and are carrying heavy burdens, and I will give you rest. Take my yoke upon you, and learn from me; for I am gentle and humble in heart, and you will find rest for your souls. For my yoke is easy, and my burden is light. (11:28–30)

"Weariness, being heavy-laden, yoke" are all ways of speaking of the commodity society of endless productivity. In context, this might have referred to the strenuous taxation system of the Roman Empire, for "yoke" often refers to imperial imposition. Alternatively, this may have referred to the endless requirements of an over-coded religious system that required endless attentiveness. With reference to imperial imposition or over-coded religion, Jesus offers an alternative: come to me and rest! He becomes the embodiment of Sabbath rest for those who are no longer defined by and committed to the system of productiveness. In this role he is, as he is characteristically, fully in sync with the tradition of Israel and with the Sabbath God who occupies that tradition.

III

Because Jews and Christians continue to attend to these commandments as contemporary mandates, we may consider the ways in which the first commandment (concerning the emancipatory God and no other) and the second commandment (concerning images as commodities) pertain to our common life. Of course, the commandments always pertain to the constancy of the human condition and to gospel possibility. But we may more particularly consider the peculiar and immediate ways that the first two commandments pertain to our present circumstances. The "choice of gods" is, in context, a choice of restlessness or restfulness.

The reality of restlessness in our contemporary society is obvious and epidemic. The identification of that restlessness perhaps goes back to the categories of Martin Luther concerning "faith and works," with the accent on "works" indicating a need to produce, perform, and qualify for the goodness of God. It is an easy move to take that Reformation accent on "works" and see in our current social restlessness evidence of not yet being good enough or having done enough. Or perhaps such restlessness is rooted in the Enlightenment discovery of the individual and the emergent ideology of individualism that cuts us off from the buoyant sustenance of community and tradition. In that ideology, one is not only free to secure one's own future without answering to any other; one is also required to secure one's own future, because a laissez-faire economics mandates that one must sink or swim by one's own effort, and it is never enough simply to tread water.

These rootages in Reformation and Enlightenment categories have created a contemporary circumstance in our society that generates an endless pursuit of greater security and greater happiness, a pursuit that is always unsatisfied, because we have never gotten or done enough . . . yet. The gods ("other gods") of this system are the gods of market ideology that summon to endless desires and needs that are never met but that always require yet greater effort.

The various elements of that restlessness of "not enough yet" and "greater effort required" are evident everywhere. But they are grounded in a theological desire for an ultimate reality of total satiation that is no reality at all. That theological "mis-commitment" is apparent in economic performance that can never fully satisfy. Such an intrinsic and systemic inadequacy is a recognizable echo of the ancient Hebrew slaves, harassed by many supervisors and taskmasters who kept reminding them of the inadequacy of their production.

The advertising game, the liturgy of consumerism in the service of market theology, always offers one more product for purchase, one more car, one more deodorant, one more prescription drug, one more cell phone, one more beer. The message is that the "product" will make one safe or simply acceptable. But the preliminary message is that one is not yet safe or not yet acceptable because one does not yet have the product. The production of "new and improved," the endless advance of style, and the always-new technology make old possessions inadequate and incomplete, so that there is and must be an open-ended effort to satisfy the gods of commodity.

In order to have economic leverage to pursue such commodity, *an educational advantage* is all but indispensable. As a result, there is a striving for improvement reflected in "teaching to the test" so that we may demonstrate not only competence but also superiority. Such a commoditization of education means that the study of tradition in artful, critical fashion is lost in the urge of test scores. In order that one may test well, moreover, there is an incessant pressure for admission to the right school and thus tutorial pressure to enhance performance.

But because test scores are not sufficient for admission to the "best" educational programs, there must be *supplementary extracurricular activity*. This in turn requires constantly attentive parents who perform as chauffeurs to get to the next tennis or soccer or piano lesson so that a prospect for fun or nurture disappears into restlessness that becomes a process of accumulation of qualifying marks.

And if young persons are cast as performers of social restlessness, the economy is a process of getting ahead or of staying even by the same route of accumulation. As a result, the restlessness becomes *a political effort* to own and control congress and court appointments in order that laws may be enacted concerning credit and tax arrangements and regulatory agencies to make way for predation by the strong and well-connected in their desire for more. That restlessness inevitably has resulted in many "left behind," who cannot compete due to poor circumstance or opportunity, or a defeatism that properly assesses one's hopeless chances in a rapacious system. The outcome of such endless striving for more is a social arrangement of the safety and happiness of the few at the expense of the many, a replica of the "pyramid" of ancient Pharaoh.

Such economic advantage and the unsustainable standard of living that it permits require *an expansive and aggressive military* in order to control resources and markets so that the world economy, reflected in the World Bank and the International Monetary Fund, is designed to keep the gains flowing to the top of the pyramid of power and success. It is not accidental that the best graphic portrayal of this arrangement is a pyramid, the supreme construction of Pharaoh's system. Those at the top require huge amounts of cheap labor at a parsimonious "minimum wage" to make such a life possible.

This limitless pursuit of consumer goods (and the political, cultural, and military requirements that go with it) in the interest of satiation necessitates overproduction and *abuse of the land*, and the squandering of limited supplies of oil and water. Thus, the environment is savaged by such restlessness, perhaps beyond viability. It is long since forgotten that rest is the final marking of creator and creation.

The totem for such restlessness is perhaps *professional sports* (with major college sports only a subset of professional sports). The endless carnival of those sports constitutes a dramatic affirmation of power, wealth, and virility in which "victory" is accomplished by many abusive exploitations, all in pursuit of winning and being on top of the heap of the money game.

And of course, every facet of this restlessness is grounded in and produces anxiety that variously issues in aggression and finally manifests in *violence*:

- violence expressed in military adventurism that enjoys huge "patriotic" support;
- violence against the earth that is signaled by overuse;
- violence in sports, now with evidence of "paid injuries";
- violence in the neighborhood, with guns now the icon of "violent security";
- violence against every vulnerable population, sexual aggression against the young, and the "war on the poor," which is accomplished by law and by banking procedures.

It is impossible, is it not, to overestimate the level of anxiety that now characterizes social relationships in our society of acute restlessness. That violent restlessness makes neighborliness nearly impossible.

None of this is new; all of it is much chronicled among us. All of it is as old as Pharaoh's Egypt. The narrative of the exodus is not a one-off miracle. The portrayal of the slave camps of Egypt and the deliverance of the exodus do not constitute an isolated miracle. The narrative is a rendering of recurring social relationships legitimated by antineighborly gods who give warrant, in the interest of commodity, to redefine neighbors as slaves, threats, rivals, and competitors.

Only when we ponder the "other gods" and the systems they authorize can we appreciate the radical nature of these first two commandments. Into this arena of restlessness comes the God of rest, who offers relief from that anxiety-producing system. This God has no hunger for commodities and does not legitimate commodity systems. This God is attentive rather to the cries of those "left behind" and comes to open futures by exit (exodus) from systems of restlessness into the restfulness of neighborliness.

The two commandments go beneath social performance and social appearance to the deep, elemental, defining issue of "God versus the gods." These gods of commoditization for the most part go unchallenged in our world. As a result, their exploitative systems go unchallenged and unnoticed. The abuse becomes normal. Restlessness is unexceptional. Anxiety is a given, and violence is unexamined as "the cost of doing business." It is all a virtual reality in which we become narcotized into a system that seems to be a given rather than a construction.

In that context, we have the exodus narrative that shows those gods of commodity to be powerless and without authority. They are phonies that we should neither fear nor serve nor trust:

> They have mouths, but do not speak;
>   eyes, but do not see.
> They have ears, but do not hear;
>   noses, but do not smell.
> They have hands, but do not feel;
>   feet, but do not walk;
>   they make no sound in their throats.
>   Ps. 115:5–7

More than that:

> Those who make them are like them;
>   so are all who trust in them.
>   v. 8

They are the ones who champion anxiety and affirm restlessness. The adherents to the gods of restlessness find such a predatory society normal.

And then into our midst comes this other unexpected voice from outside the Pharaonic system: "Let my people go!" (Exod. 5:1). It is not surprising that Pharaoh does not recognize the commanding voice of YHWH. Pharaoh's system precludes and denies any such commanding voice that emancipates (v. 2). But YHWH persists: Let them go outside the system of restlessness that ends in violence. Let them depart the system of endless production, in order to enter a world of covenantal fidelity. In ancient context, they must depart from the Egyptian system in order to dance and sing freedom.

The departure from that same system in our time is not geographical. It is rather emotional, liturgical, and economic. It is not an idea but a practical act. Thus the Sabbath of the fourth commandment is an act of trust in the subversive, exodus-causing God of the first commandment, an act of submission to the restful God of commandments one, two, and three. Sabbath is a practical divestment so that neighborly engagement, rather than production and consumption, defines our lives. It is for good reason that Sabbath has long been, for theologically serious Jews, the defining discipline. It is also for good reason that Enlightenment-based autonomous Christians may find the Sabbath commandment the most urgent and the most difficult of all the commandments of Sinai. We are, liberals and conservatives, much inured to Pharaoh's system. For that reason, the departure into restfulness is both urgent and difficult, for our motors are set to run at brick-making speed. To cease, even for a time, the anxious striving for more bricks is to find ourselves with a "light burden" and an "easy yoke." It is now, as then, enough to permit dancing and singing into an alternative life.

Questions for Reflection

1. The gods of productivity of Egypt are held up in stark contrast to the God of Israel, who is the God of rest and Sabbath. These gods of production move us into a world based on consumerism and a constant output of goods that supports systems of fear and anxiety. How are these gods manifest in your own life? Can you name these gods for yourself?

2. Throughout history we have seen artists' depictions of God, biblical figures, and Jesus. Creating images of God can be counterproductive, or even dangerous, limiting the imagination and creativity of YHWH. Can you think of some of these images? Look them up. Study them. How might they limit our view of God? What makes this dangerous? At the same time, God in the exodus and throughout the Bible is an embodied God, manifest and at work in and through the material conditions of creation. How have images of God and other material things helped you know and experience God's presence and work in the world?

3. The images of God that emerge out of contexts that demand endless productivity tend to be mouthpieces for these demands. The consequences of devotion to such deities typically involve dissatisfaction with oneself for not being productive enough and unhealthy relations with others, who are seen either as competitors or as a means to enhance one's productivity. In what ways does your context reflect a demand for endless productivity? What consequences have you experienced as a result? A desire for constant stimulation? Comparison with others? Aggression? Violence?

4. Having named, pondered, and analyzed our own gods and the limits we place on God, how do we turn from these things and live into the first two commandments? What are practical ways we can carry out the task of Sabbath and rest?

Chapter 4

The Central Commandment

Sabbath Abundance and the Holy Zone of the Tabernacle

*W*hen Israel arrives at Sinai, a new, extended, complex tradition begins, featuring (a) the making of *covenant* between YHWH and Israel, and (b) the issuance of the *commands* of YHWH that become the condition and substance of the covenant. The history and geographic location of Sinai remain unknown. The importance of the mountain lies instead in the decisive role it plays in Israel's paradigmatic story of salvation as the site for many, varied, and complex traditions of laws and customs that sought to extend the rule and will of YHWH to every aspect of life, personal and public, civic and cultic. Within the framework of Israel's paradigmatic story of salvation, the new commands at Sinai give shape to YHWH's dream that Israel organize its social life for the common good, in contrast with the scarcity system from which they departed.

I

Israel arrives at Sinai in Exodus 19:1, which begins a section of materials from Exodus 19–24 that scholars commonly term the "Sinai pericope." These chapters include a preparation for the meeting with YHWH at the mountain (19:10–25), the proclamation of the Ten Commandments (20:1–17), the acceptance of Moses as the normative mediator of Torah (vv. 18–21), and a concluding narrative of covenant making, whereby Israel takes an oath of allegiance to YHWH (chap. 24). The *proclamation of commands* and the *oath of allegiance* are the defining elements of the covenant that bind Israel to YHWH

in obedience. While it is not possible to establish the early date of the
Ten Commandments, it is readily seen that this catalog of commands
is the most elemental of all of YHWH's Torah requirements. In a
sense, all the other commands are interpretations of these ten.

- From commandments 1–3, Israel learned that YHWH is to be
  loved, served, and trusted, rather than Pharaoh's security system:

> I am the LORD your God, who brought you out of the land
> of Egypt, out of the house of slavery; you shall have no
> other gods before me.
>   You shall not make for yourself an idol, whether in the
> form of anything that is in heaven above, or that is on the
> earth beneath, or that is in the water under the earth. You
> shall not bow down to them or worship them; for I the
> LORD your God am a jealous God, punishing children for
> the iniquity of parents, to the third and the fourth genera-
> tion of those who reject me, but showing steadfast love to
> the thousandth generation of those who love me and keep
> my commandments.
>   You shall not make wrongful use of the name of the
> LORD your God, for the LORD will not acquit anyone who
> misuses his name. (Exod. 20:2–7)

As we saw in chapter 3, these three commandments are nothing less
than regime change; they declare that there is an alternative to the
anxiety-producing enterprise of Pharaoh. The command is to worship
the one who liberates from Pharaoh, and to honor the inscrutable holiness of the God who will not be squeezed into any production system.

- Israel learned, from commandments 5–9, that neighbors, all kinds
  of neighbors, are to be respected, protected, and not exploited:

> Honor your father and your mother, so that your days may
> be long in the land that the LORD your God is giving you.
>   You shall not murder.
>   You shall not commit adultery.
>   You shall not steal.
>   You shall not bear false witness against your neighbor.
> (vv. 12–16)

These terse rules set a boundary on the way in which the neighbor can be "used." Pharaoh, of course, knew no such boundaries, but was free to manage and manipulate neighbors in any way at all, in order to increase production. At Sinai it is clear that neighbors are ends and not means, agents in their own history and not merely cogs in a security system.

- Israel learned, from the tenth commandment, that there is a limit to acquisitiveness:

> You shall not covet your neighbor's house; you shall not covet your neighbor's wife, or male or female slave, or ox, or donkey, or anything that belongs to your neighbor.

As we will see in chapter 5, the commandment is not about petty acts of envy. It is about predatory practices and aggressive policies that make the little ones vulnerable to the ambitions of the big ones. In a rapacious economic system, nobody's house and nobody's field and nobody's wife and nobody's oil are safe from a stronger force. The exploitative system of Pharaoh believed that it always needed more and was always entitled to more—more bricks, more control, more territory, more oil—until it had everything. But of course one cannot order a neighborhood that way, because such practices and such assumptions generate only fear and competition that make the common good impossible. Such greed is prohibited by YHWH's kingdom of generosity.

- Israel learned from the fourth commandment that Sabbath rest is an alternative to aggressive anxiety:

> Remember the sabbath day, and keep it holy. Six days you shall labor and do all your work. But the seventh day is a sabbath to the LORD your God; you shall not do any work—you, your son or your daughter, your male or female slave, your livestock, or the alien resident in your towns. For in six days the LORD made heaven and earth, the sea, and all that is in them, but rested the seventh day; therefore the LORD blessed the sabbath day and consecrated it. (vv. 8–11)

Sabbath, in the first instance, is not about worship. It is about work stoppage. It is about withdrawal from the anxiety system of Pharaoh, the refusal to let one's life be defined by production and consumption and the endless pursuit of private well-being. It is easy to imagine that in Pharaoh's system there never was a Sabbath for anyone. Everyone was 24/7! The slaves never got a day off and perhaps had to multitask to meet their quotas. Pharaoh surely never took a day off; he was too busy writing memos and sending out work orders and quotas. As a result everyone was caught up in an endless process of production and accumulation.

But at Sinai Israel could remember from the manna narrative that, although they were told not to store up bread for the next day, there was an exception to that rule made only for Sabbath:

> "See! The LORD has given you the sabbath, therefore on the sixth day he gives you food for two days; each of you stay where you are; do not leave your place on the seventh day." So the people rested on the seventh day. (Exod. 16:29–30)

What a surprise! Even in the wilderness, where there is no extra bread at all, provision is made for Sabbath. Even in the desperate context of wilderness, work stoppage is definitional because the God of Sinai wants energy invested in the neighborhood and not in self-securing in order to get ahead, as in the empire. Of course there were cheats who multitasked on Sabbath, thereby to get a leg up on bread. But the provision of Sinai is otherwise; Sabbath is an occasion for community enhancement, for eating together and remembering and hoping and singing and dancing and telling stories—all exercises that have no production value. Israel learned at Sinai, and most especially in the fourth command on Sabbath, that there is a viable way to organize the neighborhood outside the rat race.

II

We may be sure that there was no seventh day in the empire, no Sabbath, no day blessed and made rich with vitality, no holy day devoted to YHWH, the Lord of the Sabbath. Seen in this way, Israel's eagerness for the Sinai commands in Exodus 19:8 is easy to understand.

The Sinai offer was an alternative to the quota system of the empire. Now the production system would be interrupted and shut down every seventh day. Israel would rest as it never did in Egypt, because YHWH, unlike the Egyptian gods, is a God of restfulness.

The fourth command at Sinai in Exodus 20:8–11 clearly refers to the litany of creation in Genesis 1:1–2:4a. That account of reality is in a symmetrical order with a repeated verdict of "good." The human couple, female and male, is charged with supervisory management of the fruitfulness system, to care, to maximize its fruitfulness, and to be sure that the generativity of the creator is reflected in the abundance of creation.

The creator God, the litany attests, is a God of blessing, capable of assigning life and well-being to every aspect of creation. By word and by act, the creator God transposed seething chaotic matter into an ordered, coherent life-support system. God transposes reality by three times blessing the creation:

- The first blessing is toward sea monsters and winged creatures:

    God blessed them, saying, "Be fruitful and multiply and fill the waters in the seas, and let birds multiply on the earth." (Gen. 1:22)

- The second blessing is toward the human couple:

    God blessed them, and God said to them, "Be fruitful and multiply, and fill the earth and subdue it; and have dominion over the fish of the sea and over the birds of the air and over every living thing that moves upon the earth." (v. 28)

- The third blessing is of the seventh day now made holy:

    So God blessed the seventh day and hallowed it, because on it God rested from all the work that he had done in creation. (Gen. 2:3)

The blessing, the infusion of the life force of God, is in turn to (a) nonhuman creatures, especially sea monsters—thus, a witness that God has ordered even chaotic waters; (b) humans as God's regents in the maintenance of an order of abundance; and (c) a day of rest intrinsic to the structure of the created order of fruitfulness.

And God rested! God had done enough. God was tired. It was the weariness of a kingly ruler who had spent a week issuing orders and edicts. It is the weariness of a caregiver who has been using energy to infuse creation with the energy of life. The fatigue of God is replicated by Jesus in the narrative of the woman who has hemorrhaged for twelve years:

> Immediately aware that power had gone forth from him, Jesus turned about in the crowd and said, "Who touched my clothes?" And his disciples said to him, "You see the crowd pressing in on you; how can you say, 'Who touched me?'" He looked all around to see who had done it. But the woman, knowing what had happened to her, came in fear and trembling, fell down before him, and told him the whole truth. (Mark 5:30–33)

Being a healer is costly to the one who heals. Being a creator is costly in the extension of blessing. Being a caregiver is costly, as every caregiver notices, because it entails the transmission of the self to the other.

But imagine: *God rested!* God rested because God was weary. This, of course, does not fit with the God of the catechism, who is beyond all such pathos in omniscience, omnipresence, and omnipotence. Such a God never rests:

> He will not let your foot be moved;
>   he who keeps you will not slumber.
> He who keeps Israel
>   will neither slumber nor sleep.
>   Ps. 121:3–4

Such a God is never depleted, never spent, never needs a day off, because such a God is not intimately and intrinsically linked to needy creation. And then, of course, it is only a small step to be made in the direction of the Promethean God of classical theology who never rests. So the pastor, caregiver, in the image of the Promethean divine caregiver, never rests, never is depleted, never is needy, is alert 24/7 in piety and devotion and self-giving because the church needs such servants. And we act with a theology of incessant availability.

But not this God! This God rests! This God so rests that Israel in its poetic imagination can entertain the thought of YHWH's dormancy. Indeed Israel can issue a wake-up call to God:

> Awake, awake, put on strength,
>   O arm of the LORD!
> Awake, as in days of old,
>   the generations of long ago!
> Was it not you who cut Rahab in pieces,
>   who pierced the dragon?
>
> Isa. 51:9

The summons in Isaiah 51 is to the creator God, the one who had in ancient times dealt with evil sea monsters. God rests because the world will work, because the tasks of creation have been delegated, and because creation, blessed as it is, knows the will and energy of the Creator and does not need constant attention. God rests, because God engages in self-care and because God has complete confidence in the sustaining energy of creation. And there came a silence over heaven and earth and the radishes said to the porcupines, "Shhh—be quiet because 'Himself' is resting, and we must tiptoe until Sunday morning when we will arise after rest to new life." The rest of the Creator causes serenity in creation. The creatures, like the Creator, are competent and trusting and unhasting. The world works and all is well.

It is, of course, to be noticed that in the liturgy of creation there is no Sabbath rest declared for the human creatures in their supervisory capacity. Are they to work 24/7 in order that creation may function properly? We may only infer. The human creature, in Godlike responsibility, is in the image of God. It belongs to the image of this God—not the Promethean God of self-sufficiency as offered in too much theology—to be weary, to be depleted, to need rest, to be secure and confident about the working of creation. It belongs to the image to reflect the Sabbath of the Creator, and where it is not so reflected, the image is violated and distorted.

Another text that concerns us may initially strike readers as odd, namely, the instruction that God gives to Moses in Exodus 25–31 about the construction of the tabernacle, a holy place for the indwelling of God. This text reflects the tedious punctiliousness of priestly perception that sounds like a building committee or a hard-working hymnal committee. This long instruction, moreover, is answered in Exodus 35–40, which is largely repetition, reporting that Moses implemented in careful detail the instructions for the holy place given at Sinai.

The text concerns us for a simple, single reason. Scholars have in recent time noticed that the long text of Exodus 25–31 is all YHWH addressed to Moses, but in seven speeches:[1]

> The LORD said to Moses. (25:1)
> The LORD spoke to Moses. (30:11)
> The LORD spoke to Moses. (30:17)
> The LORD spoke to Moses. (30:22)
> The LORD said to Moses. (30:34)
> The LORD spoke to Moses. (31:1)
> The LORD said to Moses. (31:12)

(The variation between "spoke" and "said" is the variation of two Hebrew verbs, *dabar* and *'amar*, but the variation is insignificant.) When we notice the number seven, we pay attention. The first six speeches of YHWH to Moses are instructions about holy place and holy ordination. Not surprisingly, it is the seventh speech of Exodus 31:12–17 that interests us. That text is no longer interested in either space or ordination; rather, the priestly imagination culminates, yet again, as in Genesis 2:1–4a, in holy time:

> You yourself are to speak to the Israelites: "You shall keep my sabbaths, for this is a sign between me and you throughout your generations, given in order that you may know that I, the LORD, sanctify you. You shall keep the sabbath, because it is holy for you; everyone who profanes it shall be put to death; whoever does any work on it shall be cut off from among the people. Six days shall work be done, but the seventh day is a sabbath of solemn rest, holy to the LORD." (Exod. 31:13–15)

Given seven speeches that culminate in Sabbath, scholars draw the inescapable conclusion that this long text is an intentional play on Genesis 1. Only now the work of creation is not cosmic; rather it is the holy place where YHWH is assured a locus of dignity and order that contradicts the disorder of chaos all around in the exile, the likely time of the formation of the text. If the text means to signify reliable God-given order, it means that the priests offer an imaginative construction of a creation as holy place that contradicts the disorder of exile. A new imaginative construct culminates with the Sabbath, for the Sabbath is a sign of the effective governance of the creator God, humans acting out of confidence that the world works and does not depend upon our frantic ceaseless activity.

This seventh speech culminates with reference to the divine Sabbath:

> It is a sign forever between me and the people of Israel that in six days the LORD made heaven and earth, and on the seventh day he rested. (Exod. 31:17)

And then, in a quirky conclusion, the text adds, "and was refreshed." That is, the Lord "rested, and was refreshed."

This is a stunning theological statement! The Hebrew uses the term *nephesh*, which occurs often in the Old Testament as a noun meaning "self" and often rendered as "soul," as in "bless the LORD, O my soul." But here the term *nephesh* is a reflexive verb; YHWH "was *nepheshed*." This odd sort of usage occurs only in two other places in the biblical text. It is used in a parallel kind of way in Exodus 23:12 with reference to the Sabbath:

> Six days you shall do your work, but on the seventh day you shall rest, so that your ox and your donkey may have relief, and your homeborn slave and the resident alien may be refreshed.

Here the reflexive verb *nephesh* pertains to "you and your ox and your donkey and your slave and your resident alien." The list is comprehensive and inclusive. Sabbath is for all parts of the household. All shall rest, for all are depleted. And in the Sabbath all— slaves, immigrants, oxen, and asses—*recover their nephesh*. All are *re-nepheshed* back to full, glad creatureliness. The other usage of this verbal form is in 2 Samuel 16:14, now more related to quotidian life and not something as high-powered as Sabbath. David is fleeing for his life from his son Absalom. He retreats to the Jordan valley:

The king and all the people who were with him arrived weary at the Jordan; and there he refreshed himself.

David and his company are depleted by fear, by anxiety, by haste, by insecurity. They are weary with a deep dread, exhausted by having lost their secure grip on a secure world. And now they are *re-nepheshed*, perhaps by cool bathing and being in a safe place, no doubt finding food. The image is important because it suggests that our *naphshim* ("selves"), our inmost identity, are on a spectrum of refreshment and exhaustion, of life and death. We regularly have our *nephesh* diminished and then recovered, and it requires pause from anxiety in order to recover the full self.

Sabbath is a time for being *re-nepheshed*, for recovery of full self by withdrawal from all that drains and exhausts and depletes. And so for God. Because of God's own life and God's own time and God's own experience, God has ordered, in the very fabric of creation, that there are limits to the demands and expectations that are to be placed on our *naphshim*.

Thus, Sabbath is about recovered *nephesh*, and *nephesh* is not a "religious idea," no "soul," but self in all of its complex social existence. That is why we might say, "You Cannot Fool Your *Nephesh*." We say often, "You can't fool your body." Of course not, but the *nephesh* more so, for *nephesh* is that intertwined complexity of all things, spiritual, moral, mental, bodily, and material, the whole self, the true self. And it will not be lied to. There are limits because we are in the image of the God who is limited to six days of energy. We are often depleted like God, and just like the ox and just like the donkey and just like a slave and just like an immigrant, we must pause. Pushed beyond that limit, the *nephesh* evaporates and creation fails. And so we must pause.

On Sabbath, we may ponder our *nephesh* in its wholeness, complexity, and social location, and imagine the voices and tasks that deplete and the voices and tasks that restore. And rest! If you need a guide for *nephesh*-pondering, try Psalm 35:

Say to *my soul*,
   "I am your salvation."
Ps. 35:3b, emphasis added

Then *my soul* shall rejoice in the LORD,
   exulting in his deliverance.
All my bones shall say,
   "O LORD, who is like you?
You deliver the weak
   from those too strong for them,
   the weak and needy from those who despoil them."
                                                vv. 9–10

How long, O LORD, will you look on?
   Rescue me from their ravages,
   my life from the lions!
                           v. 17, emphasis added

These three uses of *nephesh* in Psalm 35 disclose a life—a *nephesh*—
that is in jeopardy but that is fully referred to YHWH, the one who
first breathed life on our clay and who moment by moment sustains
us. In turn the psalmist refers to his *nephesh* in order

- to seek God's promise of salvation
- to anticipate praise and thanks toward God
- to petition for rescue of life from the lions

   These uses altogether suggest a life—this life, every life, my life,
your life—complex and at risk, jostled, threatened, unappreciated,
in jeopardy, returning to the creator redeemer God who is the only
source of solace or protection. So imagine your *nephesh*, the one
weary every Sunday, the one assaulted nearly every day, the one
celebrated and adored at birth, the one commuting regularly between
hurt and well-being; imagine this *nephesh* depleted. In our depletion
our *nephesh* is like the *nephesh* of God, and we must rest!
   What a piece of literary architecture, that Exodus 25–31 imagines
and construes a safe, ordered place where the holiness of God can
touch down without pollution or disturbance. Except that at the last
moment, in the seventh speech, the promise of space, in characteristic Jewish fashion, is converted to a safe, ordered time for rehabilita-
tion. In this regard, the tabernacle-to-Sabbath sequence is exactly
parallel to Genesis 1, which ponders fruitful space for six days and at
the last moment turns to holy time.

On the follow-up obedience of Exodus 35–40, where Moses constructs what was commanded, the work is completed. The space and the time are in order, and the narrator reports:

> In this way all the work of the tabernacle of the tent of meeting was *finished*; the Israelites had done everything just as the LORD had commanded Moses. (39:32, emphasis added)

> He set up the court around the tabernacle and the altar, and put up the screen at the gate of the court. So Moses *finished* the work. (40:33, emphasis added)

It is finished! It is constituted! Holy zone where God dwells! Holy time where *nephesh* sits down! Holy space and holy time, holy life devoted to the presence of God and healing, and a vision of God's glory come among us—full of grace and truth—God's glory that we are to practice and enjoy. This space is unlike any other space. This time is unlike any other time. This life is unlike any other life. It is this space and this time and this life that stand as the wellness center of creation. There is no substitute, no reasonable facsimile, no adequate trade-off or compensation. An act of restful restoration engages the character of the Creator, even as it is engraved in the life of the creation; imagine, moreover, that we are made in that image to turn from busyness to restfulness and so back to full joyous creatureliness, the kind intended by the Creator. It is the truth of our life that we are meant for restful restoration.

III

The Creator promises and guarantees abundance, and Sabbath is the day we luxuriate in that abundance as a gift that we do not need to perform or possess or acquire or achieve . . . because it is a gift! But of course, we do not keep Sabbath, and so violate the inviolate reality of our God-given *naphshim*. And why? Well, I propose: we violate Sabbath and so diminish and deplete our *naphshim* because *we do not believe in, trust in, or count on God's abundance.* We do not think that creation is abundant, and we do not trust the guarantee of the Creator. The outcome of such distrust, I propose, is a devouring anxiety . . . just as Sabbath is a total antidote to anxiety. For what remains, I juxtapose Sabbath and anxiety. Note well "anxiety" . . . not "sin" or "guilt"!

When we do not trust in guaranteed abundance, we must supply the deficiencies out of our own limited resources. We scramble to move from our sense of scarcity to an abundance that we imagine we ourselves can supply, all the while frantically anxious that we won't quite make it:

- Not enough to be loved
- Not enough to be well liked
- Not enough to advance
- Not enough to secure my family
- Not enough members
- Not enough dollars
- Not enough published articles
- Not enough new clothes, new cars, new houses
- Not enough bombs
- Not enough stocks and bonds
- Not enough freedom
- Not enough purity
- Not enough of our kind of people

It is necessary to erode the holy time of Sabbath for the sake of productivity, given our sense of scarcity grounded in distrust. Yet the guarantee of God's abundance makes our anxiety unnecessary, because it is a gift, the gift of the gospel, which is more powerful than our nightmares.

The Israelites departed Sinai with a new possibility. They were able to dream of enough for all, a dream that refused the common and recurring nightmares of scarcity. To be sure, there is enough yet in ancient Israel of violence and exploitation of all kinds. But now the word has been uttered; the bread has been given and broken; the commandments have been received; the Sabbath has been celebrated. Israel and its allies in covenant have stayed on the path away from Pharaoh and toward the neighborhood. Eventually the Torah was moved from Sinai to Jerusalem. In Jerusalem came new poets who extended the covenantal vision of the common good that had been ceded at Sinai. For out of Sinai, via Jerusalem, has come a rich scenario of the common good, of peaceable well-being:

In days to come
the mountain of the LORD's house
shall be established as the highest of the mountains,
and shall be raised up above the hills.
Peoples shall stream to it,
and many nations shall come and say:
"Come, let us go up to the mountain of the LORD,
to the house of the God of Jacob;
that he may teach us his ways
and that we may walk in his paths."
For out of Zion shall go forth instruction,
and the word of the LORD from Jerusalem.
He shall judge between many peoples,
and shall arbitrate between strong nations far away;
they shall beat their swords into plowshares,
and their spears into pruning hooks;
nation shall not lift up sword against nation,
neither shall they learn war any more;
but they shall all sit under their own vines and under their own
fig trees,
and no one shall make them afraid;
for the mouth of the LORD of hosts has spoken.

Mic. 4:1–4

It is all of a piece! There is an alternative! Recipients of overwhelming abundance can redirect their energies away from fearful anxiety to investment in the common good of the neighborhood.

From these texts we draw these peculiar claims:

- Persons living in *a system of anxiety and fear*—and consequently greed—have no time or energy for the common good. Defining anxiety focuses total attention on the self at the expense of our *naphshim* and the common good.
- *An immense act of generosity* is required in order to break the death grip of the system of fear, anxiety, and greed.
- Those who are immersed in such immense gifts of generosity are able to get their minds off themselves, recover their *nephesh*, and can be *about the work of the neighborhood*. Children of such enormous abundance are able to receive new commandments that are about the well-being of the neighborhood and not about the entitlements of the self.

Questions for Reflection

1. Sabbath was instilled in the culture of Israel at Sinai as a means to stop work and to invest in the neighborhood. This investment was intended, not to perpetuate the systems of the empire and Pharaoh, but to enhance the community apart from economic production. Are you observing Sabbath in this way? Create a list of the ways in which you can create Sabbath so that your community is enriched through mutuality.

2. God speaks to Moses on Mount Sinai in seven speeches that culminate in the reassurance that God, as a God of rest, effectively governs creation. Creation, then, is not based on frantic and ceaseless activity and production. How does this change the way in which you move through your life? Your work life? Your ministry? Are you ready to move into a new concept of creation that involves Sabbath so that you may be refreshed?

3. Our lives, our *nephesh*, are constantly being bombarded with voices and forces that deplete and restore. Take some time right now to think about and compose a list of the things that deplete your *nephesh*. Now, compose a list of the things that restore your *nephesh*. Consider continuing to add to these lists in order to remind yourself to cultivate this holy space of restoration.

4. The task of curbing the anxious and fear-driven systems of productivity is not an easy one. Anxiety creeps into our *nephesh* and we often wonder if we are enough. Take a moment to honestly reflect: Do you think you are enough? What are your worries about following the true Sabbath of God? What are your fears concerning leaning into a creation that reflects rest and community?

Chapter 5

The Final Commandments

Covenant without Coveting

*I*n this exploration of a biblical notion of salvation, we have followed Moses out of an anxious Egypt, through the surprising abundance in the wilderness, and to the mountain where we receive God's
instructions for organizing social life for the common benefit of the
community. The final utterance of God in the awesome confrontation
at Mount Sinai is this: "You shall not covet" (Exod. 20:17). It is as
though this fearsome God has saved the sharpest zinger for this final
statement. This terse prohibition seems an appropriate pivot point
to the core narrative of ancient Israel that was repeatedly reiterated
in many variations in Israel. The narrative begins in the wondrous
creation lyric of Genesis 1 that culminates in Sabbath (Gen. 2:1–4).
It sweeps through the ancestral narratives of Genesis, the emancipation from Egypt, the brief narrative of wilderness sojourn, the defining confrontation at Sinai, and more travel to the edge of the land of
promise. James Sanders has noticed that the normative text of the
Torah (Pentateuch) does not bring Israel into the land of promise but
only to the entry point.[1] We might imagine with Michael Fishbane
that the narrative account is from "Adamic" humanity to "Mosaic"
humanity, that is, from creation to Sinai.[2] If we trace this movement
from Adam to Moses, we may suggest that the core story is a story
about coveting. At least this is one possible rendering that serves our
topic of biblical salvation as emancipation from anxiety and exploitation and for the flourishing of the common good.

This tenth commandment refers to an originary attitude of desire,
of being propelled in ways we do not understand to desire what is
not properly our own, so that desire becomes a powerful, seductive

force that skews one's life. The commandment suggests that it is the stuff that the neighbor has (wife, house, anything) that evokes the seductive energy of desire. It requires, moreover, no great imagination to see that our current consumer society is much propelled by such desire, which is in part natural but also is in some great part manufactured.

The history of desire surely runs, in Christian tradition, all the way from Augustine to Adam Smith. Augustine is the great theologian of desire; he himself felt and noticed the compelling power of objects that become seductive and distorting of life.[3] He recognized that our true desire is for God, but that distorted desire focuses on many lesser objects that interrupt a proper desire for God. In the modern world, Adam Smith, in his analysis of "sentiment," noticed the way in which human persons can be propelled by wants; he observed further that such wants can be intentionally managed or manipulated.[4] Thus the history of coveting, in the memory and tradition of ancient Israel, is the story of proper desire and distorted desire that causes a confusion of proper desire and distorted wanting. It is a story that continues among us.

I

The tenth commandment, however, is misunderstood when it is taken, as it often is, as though it simply concerns an attitude of envy. Thus the tenth commandment is sometimes taken as very different from the other nine because the other nine clearly concern action, while this tenth one concerns attitude. The misunderstanding occurs because the term "covet" in truth concerns not only an attitude of *wanting* but also an action of *taking*. Thus it concerns, like the other nine commandments, actual behavior. The prohibition concerns the acquiring of what belongs to another. The combination of *wanting* (*desiring*) and *seizing* (*acquiring*) produces an acquisitive system of wealth that is self-propelled until it becomes an addiction that skews viable social relationships so that no one is safe from predatory eagerness.

The tenth commandment, moreover, suggests, on the one hand, that such wanting/taking is prohibited, because it is contrary to the

will of the God of Sinai. The God of the gospel does not intend
that social life should consist in the unrestrained, addictive pursuit
of commodities. But on the other hand, as always in the Bible,
the practical expression of the divine prohibition is the presence
of the neighbor.[5] The term "neighbor" occurs three times in this
terse commandment, and it is the first usage in the Decalogue, as
though this is the originary statement of a faith perspective that
finally concerns the well-being of the neighbor. It is the reality
of the neighbor that is the God-acknowledged check on addictive acquisitiveness. The neighbor is a line that must not be trans-
gressed, because the neighbor is an undeniable social fact that
will not go away. Acknowledgment of the neighbor, the neighbor's presence, and the neighbor's property is indispensable for a
viable social order. As the tradition develops, moreover, special
emphasis is placed on the vulnerable neighbors who are without
guaranteed social rights or the protection of an effective advocate.
Thus the tradition of Deuteronomy, the great neighbor manifesto,
asserts: "You must not move your neighbor's boundary marker,
set up by former generations, on the property that will be allotted
to you in the land that the LORD your God is giving you to possess" (Deut. 19:14).

The same prohibition is expressed in the wisdom tradition:

> Do not remove an ancient landmark
>   or encroach on the fields of orphans,
> for their redeemer is strong;
>   he will plead their cause against you.
>   Prov. 23:10–11; see 22:28

Coveting is inimical to viable community. The prohibition in the
commandment anticipates the capacity of the rich and powerful, with
smart lawyers, to override the unprotected claims of the vulnerable.
From the outset, Israel from Sinai has to work to construct an alternative economy in which desire is limited by neighbor and confiscation
is limited by divine prohibition. The play on the term "redeemer" in
Proverbs 23:11 refers to an effective social advocate. But of course
theologically God, the Redeemer, is on the side of protecting the
economic viability of the vulnerable.

II

Israel, of course, has no monopoly on the temptation to covet. The history of coveting begins already in the creation narrative:

> So when the woman saw that the tree was good for food, and that it was a delight to the eyes, and that the tree was to be desired to make one wise, she took of its fruit and ate; and she also gave some to her husband, who was with her, and he ate. (Gen. 3:6)

Claus Westermann has observed that this verse joins together two quite different ideas.[6] On the one hand, there is delight in sensual pleasure; the fruit was pleasing. The attraction was intensified by being prohibited. Westermann's judgment is that this in itself is not taken as unnatural desire. Attraction to pleasing sensual objects is natural. On the other hand, the desire to make one's self wise, that is, "to rise above one's self," to achieve "new possibilities of life," is the core temptation. It is the desire to transcend one's self by seizing what is not one's own that is the act of coveting. Such coveting is a refusal to accept the limitations of one's self and to imagine that such limitation (in this narrative God-given) can be transcended. This is the "Adamic man" of whom Fishbane writes.

In reading through the ancestral narratives, we may mention that Abraham, recipient of the promise of land, in Genesis 13 treats his nephew Lot magnanimously. He is not covetous of land but permits Lot to choose what he will have:

> Then Abram said to Lot, "Let there be no strife between you and me, and between your herders and my herders; for we are kindred. Is not the whole land before you? Separate yourself from me. If you take the left hand, then I will go to the right; or if you take the right hand, then I will go to the left." (vv. 8–9)

By contrast, the sons of Jacob who are the brothers of Joseph surely are covetous of the status of privilege enjoyed by their younger brother (Gen. 37:18–19). In their enmity they sought to eliminate him.

III

The history of coveting finally comes to Pharaoh, who is the quintessential coveter in the imagination and memory of Israel. The note on famine in Genesis 12:10 indicates that Pharaoh already had an ample food supply. His nightmares in Genesis 41:1–7, however, evidence that Pharaoh is overcome with anxiety about food; he is frightened by the prospect of scarcity. There is surely some irony in the fact that the one with the most is the one who has dreams of scarcity. The narrative may indeed be about food. More likely, however, it is that Pharaoh himself was not yet "enough," did not control enough, and so had to take steps beyond his anxiety about his regime. His program of compensation included the designation of Joseph, a Hebrew, to administer a plan to overcome Pharaoh's anxiety and to ensure against any potential scarcity. Because Pharaoh already has a sufficient food supply, so sufficient that he could feed refugees from other places of famine, we may conclude that his anxiety was not informed by reality. It was rather propelled by an anxious resolve to be self-sufficient.

The report of Genesis 47:13–26 makes clear that there was no limit to Pharaoh's usurpatious policies. In three successive years, Joseph, on behalf of Pharaoh, reduces peasant agriculture to slavery as the crown comes to possess all of the land:

> Then Joseph said to the people, "Now that I have this day bought you and your land for Pharaoh, here is seed for you; sow the land. And at the harvests you shall give one-fifth to Pharaoh, and four-fifths shall be your own, as seed for the field and as food for yourselves and your households, and as food for your little ones." . . . So Joseph made it a statute concerning the land of Egypt, and it stands to this day, that Pharaoh should have the fifth. The land of the priests alone did not become Pharaoh's. (vv. 23–24, 26)

The generous tone of Joseph seeks to hide the economic reality that the land and its produce have been seized from the peasants for Pharaoh.

Pharaoh did indeed covet his neighbor's field and found a way to acquire it for himself by placing the peasants in an unsustainable economic position as tenant farmers. The exodus narrative that follows from Pharaoh's side is a narrative of unrelieved desire for more. Thus the slaves, who are treated ruthlessly, are kept busy with the task of building more storehouses so that Pharaoh can store the surplus grain produced by his agricultural monopoly (Exod 1:11). The picture given in the narrative is a kind of restless acquisitiveness that has no restraint at all but that simply must have more, no matter what. The confrontation in Exodus 5 gives voice to Pharaoh's endless urge to have more: more labor to make more bricks to build more granaries to store more grain to control more of the food supply (5:4–19). It is evident that such a policy of brutalizing acquisitiveness has no restraint due to the claims of the neighbor, because there were no neighbors on Pharaoh's horizon; there were only workers pressed for more productivity.

This picture of seething, coercive productivity is in stark contrast to the provision for Sabbath rest at the conclusion of the creation narrative (Gen. 2:1–3). One could conclude that the willful, limitless force of desire has made Sabbath a socioeconomic impossibility in Pharaoh's world. Such desire on Pharaoh's part is destructive of human relationships, for the slaves are reduced to a commodity, no more of value than the bricks that they produce.

The exodus narrative, read as part of the history of coveting, is thus an emancipation from the economic domain of coveting that brutalizes and dehumanizes in the compulsion for more. It is no surprise as a result that the Sabbath looms large in the community of the emancipated. Such Sabbath in time to come is not only disciplined rest. It is an active form of resistance against insatiable desire that regularly segues to brutalizing seizure.[7]

In the story of the departure of the slaves from the domain of acquisitive desire, it is reported that the Israelites did indeed take with them commodities from Pharaoh to which they were not entitled, thus also a form of possession:

> I will bring this people into such favor with the Egyptians that, when you go, you will not go empty-handed; each woman shall ask her neighbor and any woman living in the neighbor's house for jewelry of silver and of gold, and clothing, and you shall put

them on your sons and on your daughters; and so you shall plunder the Egyptians. (Exod. 3:21–22; see 11:2; 12:35–36)

It is curious that this confiscation by the slaves of the possessions of Pharaoh is passed over without comment and certainly without any criticism. Perhaps from the perspective of the emancipated such appropriation is legitimate payback for Pharaoh's inordinate seizures. The act indicates that Israel was not lacking interest in or disengaged from possessions, but had to act stealthily in the face of the overwhelming power and the confiscatory practice of Pharaoh. The emancipated were not left "empty-handed" in their departure!

IV

The emancipation of Israel from Pharaoh's Egypt was a departure from a regime of inordinate coveting. But the future after the departure was risky and not guaranteed. For good reason the emancipated slaves had an urging to return to the desire system of Pharaoh that had victimized them (Exod. 16:2–3). Since Pharaoh had monopolized all food, they were left with wonderment whether there was any viable alternative to the usurpatious system of Pharaoh. In Exodus 16, on the first leg of the trip of emancipation, the drama of risk and scarcity is acted out. They are now outside the domain of Pharaoh's monopoly. But outside the domain of monopolized commodities, they become, after much grumbling, the recipients of the inexplicable gifts of meat (v. 13), bread (vv. 14–18), and water (17:1–7). It turned out, to their relief and surprise, that outside Pharaoh's regime, the domain of monopolized commodity, a sustainable life was possible. We may reckon the manna story as being the pivotal narrative that attests a viable alternative to the kingdom of inordinate desire. Gifts are given! The place of destitution turns out to be the locus of abundance. It turns out, to the surprise of the characters in the narrative, that there is indeed life, sustainable life, outside the kingdom of acquisitive desire. We may read the narrative and respond, "Who knew?" Who knew there was life in the wilderness? Who knew there was sustenance apart from possessions? Who knew YHWH was a provider who could and would outdistance the parsimonious provisions of Pharaoh? Who knew, indeed? The abundance of YHWH is the counterpoint to the coveting of wealth and possessions in the Bible!

The narrative of manna in Exodus 16 suggests three important points in our focus here on wealth and possessions in this story of biblical salvation. First, there is enough, but it must be shared:

> This is what the LORD has commanded: "Gather as much of it as each of you needs, an omer to a person according to the number of persons, all providing for those in their own tents." The Israelites did so, some gathering more, some less. But when they measured it with an omer, those who gathered much had nothing over, and those who gathered little had no shortage; they gathered as much as each of them needed. (16:16–18)

Second, the gift food must not be stored up. They tried that. In their anxiety about sustenance, they tried to imitate Pharaoh by hoarding. But it would not work. Bread given out of inexplicable divine generosity does not function according to Pharaoh's quotas of desire:

> And Moses said to them, "Let no one leave any of it over until morning." But they did not listen to Moses; some left part of it until morning, and it bred worms and became foul. And Moses was angry with them. Morning by morning they gathered it, as much as each needed; but when the sun grew hot, it melted. (vv. 19–21)

Third, the narrative ends with provision for Sabbath rest:

> Moses said, "Eat it today, for today is a sabbath to the LORD; today you will not find it in the field. Six days you shall gather it; but on the seventh day, which is a sabbath, there will be none."
>
> On the seventh day some of the people went out to gather, and they found none. The LORD said to Moses, "How long will you refuse to keep my commandments and instructions? See! The LORD has given you the sabbath, therefore on the sixth day he gives you food for two days; each of you stay where you are; do not leave your place on the seventh day." So the people rested on the seventh day. (vv. 25–30)

In such a marginal existence one might have expected a daily, unrelieved foraging for food in the wilderness. But the creator God who governs the wilderness has provided more than enough. Even the need for food does not require the zone of YHWH's governance to become an endless rat race for more. There is, of course, something hugely ironic in this narrative:

> Pharaoh's zone of much food is endlessly restless for more.
> YHWH's zone of precarious food allows for Sabbath rest and refuses to allow the gift bread of the wilderness to be recruited for the rat race of Pharaoh.

Sabbath is a refusal of the rat race of commodity acquisition; coveting is in contradiction to the alternative of Sabbath. Or better, Sabbath is the alternative to coveting.

Thus the issue is joined in a dramatic way: the unrelieved rat race for more that is propelled by anxiety about scarcity, or a measured, disciplined work stoppage even in the wilderness, because this is a zone of YHWH's abundance. Sabbath in such an environment is a refusal to join the chase for possessions that had become all-defining for Pharaoh. The emancipatory work of YHWH provides a genuine alternative to the insatiable acquisitiveness of Pharaoh. Manna is the shorthand gospel answer to coveting. It is an affirmation that the abundance from God is more than adequate. The abundance of God in the wilderness is not unlike the abundance of God in the garden of delight where the first couple lived. In the garden they would not trust that abundance, and so they were propelled by desire that was not in sync with their situation amid generous divine provision. Now Israel has the opportunity to respond differently. The great insight of the Genesis narrative is that even the garden of abundance is host to the hissing voice of seduction. For that reason, it will not surprise that, in time to come, that same hissing voice of desire will continue to operate destructively in Israel. Indeed, already in this narrative some, in defiance of the Sabbath prohibition, nevertheless do go out to collect bread on the Sabbath!

V

Now there is a pause in the tradition for the meeting at Sinai. The textual tradition of Sinai is saturated with memories of Egypt-exodus. Thus at the outset, in Exodus 19:4–6, it is clear that Sinai is an alternative to Pharaoh's Egypt. And when God begins to delineate the Ten Commandments, the first reference is to Egypt: "I am the LORD your God, who brought you out of the land of Egypt, out of the house of slavery" (20:2).

The one who speaks is the Emancipator from the acquisitive society of Pharaoh. Indeed, the Ten Commandments by design are a counter and alternative to Pharaoh's governance.[8] Pharaoh's Ten Commandments in Exodus 5 are all commandments for "more." The Sinai commandments are a prohibition of organizing life as a pursuit of possessions. They are guidelines for how to live well and faithfully outside Pharaoh's world, which is devoted to the pursuit of possessions. The commandments are a championing of reliable, durable relationships of trust as an alternative to the pursuit of commodity. And while the term "neighbor" is not used before the tenth commandment, it is clear that the commandments are rules for honoring and sustaining neighborliness. This is a commitment and possibility that are nowhere present in Pharaoh's acquisitiveness, for acquisitiveness precludes neighborliness.

The choice of faithful relationship over commodities is defining for Israel. The deep contrast between the two is eventually echoed in Augustine's teaching that we may love persons in relationship and use commodities, whereas Pharaoh would do exactly the opposite, to use persons and love commodities.[9]

With respect to our focus on wealth and possessions in the biblical story of salvation, the Ten Commandments are regulations for refusing the endless propulsion of wanting and taking. The first commandment begins with reference to emancipation from Egypt, the land that stands in Israel's imagination as a metaphor for brutalizing coveting. And the second commandment is a loud warning against undue attention to commodities that beg for worship (20:4–6). The fourth commandment, on Sabbath, is an attestation that disciplined regular work stoppage, the kind of work stoppage not permitted by addictive acquisitiveness, is indispensable for maintaining a world of relationships of fidelity and obedience. The tenth commandment, "You shall not covet," is not as simple as it looks, but rather comes as the culmination of a long history of coveting. The commandment reaches toward each of the players in the history of coveting:

- It addresses *Adamic personhood*, the human creatures who already in the garden of abundance, in their inordinate desire, brought huge trouble for themselves. The commandment invites all such Adamic persons into the counterworld of Mosaic membership.
- It addresses *Pharaoh* by a summary condemnation of his way of governance, thus anticipating a condemnation of all rapacious economic systems and practices that are driven by anxiety about scarcity into a frantic pursuit of more.
- It has in its horizon *the neighbor*. It is the acknowledgment of the neighbor as a figure of dignity and respect that enunciates the curbing of greed. The respect for boundary of the neighbor leads eventually to the prayer "Forgive us our trespasses, as we forgive those who trespass against us." The maintenance of proper and just boundaries guarantees a viable and peaceable society.
- It attests *YHWH* as the giver of the commandment. YHWH is the God who forbids acquisitiveness that is destructive of historical possibility. The reason YHWH can prohibit such acquisitiveness is that YHWH governs in abundance from a stance of generosity. The manna narrative in which YHWH provides enough for all is Israel's great witness against scarcity.

Questions for Reflection

1. Our desires to want and then, in turn, to take, form systems that skew our relationships with ourselves and with our neighbors. Materialism and power often drive these desires. What objects in your life have skewed your relationships with your neighbors? What are the "wants" and "desires" that consume your everyday striving?

2. The coveting of Pharaoh and the constant push for productivity directly translate to our current context in which capitalist output and consumerism make it feel difficult, even impossible, to many people to fully honor and keep Sabbath. Are you feeling this impossibility right now? Why?

3. Another characteristic of Pharaoh's system is the rat race for more—the manipulation of self and others in order to keep gaining. Often, we find ourselves playing this game consciously or unconsciously. In what ways do you find yourself a player in the rat race for more?

4. Once we are outside of this game, the work to develop trusting and faithful relationships becomes central to our walk with the God of abundance. How can you begin the process of developing trusting and faithful relationships? What work can you do to practice trust?

PART THREE

Further Instructions for Well-Being

Chapter 6

Israel's Liberatory Instructions
for Alternative Community

*I*n the canonical sequence of the core narrative of Israel, the Decalogue is followed by a subset of commandments called by scholars the Book of the Covenant (Exod. 21:1–23:19).[1] It is likely that the collection was originally independent of the Decalogue; its present placement, however, permits us to consider it as a commentary on or interpretation of the Decalogue. In this chapter we begin to explore the extent to which Israel's fundamental narrative of salvation in the exodus, as well as the fundamental principles that we discovered in our examination of the Ten Commandments, provide the ground and horizon for other legal materials beyond Exodus 20. After some consideration of the Book of the Covenant, I turn to the book of Deuteronomy, which we will further examine in subsequent chapters.

I

The commandments in the Book of the Covenant are a mixed lot. From the previous chapter's focus on Israel's prohibition against coveting, we may consider three of these commandments in particular:

1. In Exodus 22:21–24 the commandment warns against oppression of the vulnerable—immigrant, orphan, widow—the great triad of the marginal who are without resources:

You shall not wrong or oppress a resident alien, for you were aliens in the land of Egypt. You shall not abuse any widow or orphan. If you do abuse them, when they cry out to me, I will surely heed their cry; my wrath will burn, and I will kill you with the sword, and your wives shall become widows and your children orphans.

Oppression is already known in Israel from Egypt; in Exodus 3:9 it is acknowledged that YHWH has seen: "The cry of the Israelites has now come to me; I have also seen how the Egyptians oppress them." Doing wrong to someone is known elsewhere in the Torah: "When an alien resides with you in your land, you shall not *oppress* the alien" (Lev. 19:33, emphasis added).

"Wrong" and "oppress" are different translations of the same Hebrew word, which concerns economic pressure on those who cannot protect themselves. Such abuse will evoke a cry of anguish and protest (on which, see Exod. 3:9). In this commandment, the accent is the assurance that YHWH not only is attentive to such a cry from the oppressed but will act vigorously in retaliation. This stipulation is an echo of the prohibition against coveting that provides for enforcement that is not voiced in the tenth commandment. Destructive action toward the neighbor evokes the anger of God.

2. In the next commandment, the concern is more explicitly economic, though the same is surely implied in 22:21–24 as well:

If you lend money to my people, to the *poor* among you, you shall not deal with them as a creditor; you shall not exact interest from them. If you take your *neighbor's* cloak in pawn, you shall restore it before the sun goes down; for it may be your *neighbor's* only clothing to use as cover; in what else shall that person sleep? And if your *neighbor* cries out to me, I will listen, for I am compassionate. (vv. 25–27, emphasis added)

Here it is the poor who are designated as the "neighbor" who is the victim of coveting. The abuse of the vulnerable poor is likely to have been legal. It concerns the ordinary process of loans with interest. In verse 26, the offense concerns collateral for a loan. With interest and collateral, the creditor of course has immense leverage over the poor, who must borrow money at whatever rate the creditor offers. The process of loan, credit, and interest is here, as always, a completely asymmetrical transaction.

Except that in the imagination of Israel, such economic transactions are never simply between creditor and debtor. They also involve YHWH, who in verse 27 speaks in the first person. The cry of the neighbor over injustice evokes the attention of YHWH, as the cry of the slaves had mobilized YHWH in the exodus narrative (Exod. 2:23–25). YHWH will listen, that is, pay attention and become involved. The ground for such attentiveness is YHWH's compassion that extends to the vulnerable. The different responses in these two regulations are perhaps complementary: the first (22:24), "I will kill you with the sword"; the second (v. 27), "I am compassionate." The two together mean that YHWH's compassion is not innocuous but has forceful implications. Of course in neither case is it said how YHWH's decisive response would occur. But even without specificity, the divine self-assertion on behalf of the vulnerable makes YHWH a force in economic transactions. The practitioners of coveting, exemplified by Pharaoh, could imagine that the powerful can act against the powerless with impunity. But no, say the commandments. It is a prohibition of great weightiness.

3. In order that we should not romanticize the significance of the Sinai regulations, we may consider another statute in the collection. Exodus 21:20–21 occurs in a list of cases that concern damage settlements for injury:

> When a slaveowner strikes a male or female slave with a rod and the slave dies immediately, the owner shall be punished. But if the slave survives a day or two, there is no punishment; for the slave is the owner's property.

In this ordinance the concern is a slave who is injured by being beaten by the slave owner as punishment. The regulation makes a closely reasoned distinction that meticulously measures the severity of the punishment administered to the slave. If the slave dies immediately from being punished, the punishment has been too severe, and the owner must be punished. We notice, however, that no particular punishment for the slave owner is delineated, even in this severe case. On the other hand, if the slave does not die the same day but lives a day or two more, this indicates that the punishment has not been too severe, and so the owner is not punished. And then the regulation adds by way of conclusion: "The slave is the owner's property." That is the NRSV translation. The slave is a commodity or a possession. But the Hebrew is even more telling; the slave is the owner's "silver," that is, money. There is no doubt that this mercenary understanding of slavery operated in our own society much too long. Slavery could not be interrupted, because the economy depended upon it. Brevard Childs comments: "It is sad to realize that this verse continued to provide a warrant for 'biblical teaching' on slavery throughout the middle of the nineteenth century in the United States."[2]

If we consider all three texts—Exodus 22:21–24; 22:25–27; and 21:20–21—it is easy enough to see that the prohibition of coveting evoked endless disputatious interpretation. The force of economic interest could cause rapacious economics to be perceived not as coveting, but only as the cost of doing business. But the testimony of the absolute prohibition stands. It is, I propose, the core confession of Israel concerning wealth and possessions, which are to be kept in the orbit of neighborliness intended by YHWH.[3]

II

Israel is to be different. This is not Adamic personhood, but now the chosen are summoned to Mosaic personhood. But of course the claim for Mosaic personhood is never clean and unambiguous. If we read in the old narrative directly from Exodus 24:18 (the end of the Sinai meeting) to 32:1, it is clear that Moses' absence evoked great anxiety in Israel. Indeed, the absence of Moses the mediator signified in Israel the absence of God. Out of that anxiety and the need for a more palpable god, Israel requests that Aaron "make gods": "Come, make gods for us, who shall go before us" (32:1).

Aaron's response indicates that *divine power* is to be equated with *valued commodity*: "Take off the gold rings that are on the ears of your wives, your sons, and your daughters, and bring them to me" (v. 2). He makes a god of gold who is credited with the exodus emancipation: "He took the gold from them, formed it in a mold, and cast an image of a calf; and they said, 'These are your gods, O Israel, who brought you up out of the land of Egypt!'" (v. 4). The newly crafted god promises security and invites offerings and sacrifices: "They rose early the next day, and offered burnt offerings and brought sacrifices of well-being; and the people sat down to eat and drink, and rose up to revel" (v. 6).

The prehistory of this text is obscure and difficult, because bull worship may have been an alternative form of YHWH worship. However that may have been, as we have the narrative, the *calf (bull) of gold* is a rival and alternative to YHWH. Divine power is readily merged or confused with self-generating wealth and possessions. The response of YHWH, and subsequently of Moses, to the "made god" of Aaron is one of alarm and then violence (vv. 7–20).

Aaron's action requires from Moses risky negotiation with YHWH, because YHWH does not look kindly on being displaced by commodity worship (Exod. 33:12–22). Divine forgiveness is required in order to begin again (34:9–10). In the new stipulations that follow from the new covenant of 34:10, there is this terse prohibition: "You shall not make cast idols."

Idols are products of valuable commodities that are transposed into objects of desire and worship. They are without passion; they command or prohibit nothing. They are easy gods that make no covenant and that have on their horizon no neighbor. They cannot practice fidelity and have no transformative power. The entire narrative of YHWH from creation through emancipation to covenant tells powerfully against such an illusionary practice of worship that is propelled by the manipulation of possessions and that has as an inescapable by-product antineighborly policy and practice. Thus the tenth commandment contra coveting is linked to the first two commandments on "only YHWH" and no idols; it is no surprise, then, that the tenth commandment focuses on neighbor, the very focus that coveting characteristically eliminates.

When we reach the narrative report of Exodus 36–40, we are in another world that reflects a very different tradition. In Exodus 25–31, Moses had received detailed instructions from God for the construction of a tabernacle as a place that may consequently host the covenant-making God. In chapters 36–40, we are told that Moses enacted precise obedience to these commands. His obedience consists in the construction of an adequate holy place. For such a construction, he must have proper building materials. Chapters 35–36 are an accounting of the accumulation of the required materials for the tabernacle construction. Moses enumerates all that he will need for the project. The people respond to his inventory in a mood of great generosity: "And they came, everyone whose heart was stirred, and everyone whose spirit was willing, and brought the LORD's offering to be used for the tent of meeting, and for all its service, and for the sacred vestments" (35:21).

The outcome of their glad generosity is a rich offering of possessions:

> So they came, both men and women; all who were of a willing heart brought brooches and earrings and signet rings and pendants, all sorts of gold objects, everyone bringing an offering of gold to the LORD. And everyone who possessed blue or purple or crimson yarn or fine linen or goats' hair or tanned rams' skins or fine leather, brought them. Everyone who could make an offering of silver or bronze brought it as the LORD's offering; and everyone who possessed acacia wood of any use in the work, brought it. (vv. 22–24)

In chapter 36, moreover, the generous offering of Israel continues: The artisans "received from Moses all the freewill offerings that the Israelites had brought for doing the work on the sanctuary. They still kept bringing him freewill offerings every morning" (36:3). Most remarkable, it is reported that the generous offerings were more than enough, more than could be used or even received:

> [A]ll the artisans who were doing every sort of task on the sanctuary came, each from the task being performed, and said to Moses, "The people are bringing much more than enough for doing the work that the LORD has commanded us to do." So Moses gave command, and word was proclaimed throughout the camp: "No man or woman is to make anything else as an offering for the sanctuary." So the people were restrained from bringing; for what they had already brought was more than enough to do all the work. (vv. 4–7)

This is one of the most amazing and most successful stewardship campaigns in the history of faith! The report is without interpretive comment. We are not told why Israel was so generous toward the Lord.

It is clear in any case that Israel did not covet. Israel did not withhold or give grudgingly. This is the antithesis of coveting. The outcome of this generous outpouring, we learn subsequently, is the construction of a tabernacle that will be occupied by the glory of

YHWH (40:34–38). In this priestly tradition, YHWH will not dwell in shabbiness or parsimony. Israel has prepared a place for the "beauty of holiness" in which wealth and possessions are devoted in singular ways to the splendor of God. Exodus 32, with its *anxious idolatry*, and Exodus 35–36, with its *unrestrained generosity*, albeit from a different interpretive tradition, present an unmistakable contrast between the *work of anxiety* that issues in self-made gods and the *work of generous self-abandonment*. Or one could judge that in both cases the people were generous. Except that in the first case, it is all self-propelled and self-making ultimacy out of what they owned. The material substance in the two narratives is the same: gold! But the gold is always situated in a narrative that determines its significance. In chapter 32, the gold is set in *a narrative of deep anxiety* and the response is an effort at self-securing. In chapters 35–36, the gold (and other precious possessions) are set in *a narrative of generous gratitude and expectation* that signals readiness for yielding to the God of the exodus.

The two narratives about wealth and possessions compete for Israel's loyalty. These two narratives of anxiety and confident trust, moreover, continue to compete among us. The narrative of anxiety will seek to control God and oppress the neighbor. The narrative of trust, to the contrary, will yield to God, to the God who stands with and by and for the neighbor. The question of competing narratives looms large and durably in the imagination of faith. Those who generously brought their wealth and possessions to the God of emancipation and covenant arrived at the assurance of the psalmist: "The LORD is my shepherd, I shall not want" (Ps. 23:1).

III

When Israel arrives at the Jordan River, perched on the banks of the promised land and eager for entry, possession, and settlement, Moses suspects a heavy dose of amnesia in the community and decides to go back to basics. He reiterates the Ten Commandments in Deuteronomy 5:6–21 with only slight variation from the statement of the Decalogue from Exodus 20. It is this statement that becomes the basis for all that follows in Deuteronomy. There are, as at Sinai, the first three commands concerning *love of God* as the holy one who will have no competitor nor be made "useful." There are, as at Sinai, the last six commands on *love of neighbor* and the protection of social relationships that are so easy to distort and exploit. All is the same at the Jordan River for Moses as it was at Sinai . . . with one big exception, the exception that concerns us here.

In Deuteronomy, Moses again places at the center of the Decalogue the Sabbath command. Now the lead imperative is not "remember" as at Sinai, but "keep" (*shamar*), a verb of more urgency that is consistent with the intense urgency of Deuteronomy. The command is the same. It concerns work stoppage:

> Observe the sabbath day and keep it holy, as the Lord your God commanded you. Six days you shall labor and do all your work. But the seventh day is a sabbath to the Lord your God. (5:12–14a)

As at Sinai, the command to work stoppage is comprehensive, including all members of the household of the stockholder, the lead male who is addressed.

But then, in most remarkable variation, Moses departs from a reiteration of the command at Sinai in two regards. First, after having mentioned "your male and female slave" in the inclusive list, he adds,

> so that your male and female slave may rest as well *as you*. (v. 14c, emphasis added)

This may also be rendered, "be like you in rest." *Be like you*! Moses— and Israel with him—is accustomed to social contrasts, class and economic distinctions. They could remember back to Egypt, wherein there was massive distinction between Egyptian power people and the slave community soon to become the people of Israel. They could remember that the privileged power people had short work hours, lots of leisure time, plenty of food, opportunity to bathe regularly and get their hair done, but the slaves worked all of the time, without leisure, had sparse food, and no baths. Indeed, they could remember that the Hebrew slave supervisors had accused Moses and Aaron of causing trouble:

They said to them, "The LORD look upon you and judge! You have brought us into bad odor with Pharaoh and his officials, and have put a sword in their hand to kill us." (Exod. 5:21)

They had called attention to slaves by seeking their freedom, and now it was said in the empire, "These people smell bad." They remembered these powerful social distinctions. And behind that, they could remember the narrative of father Joseph that the Egyptians ate separate from Joseph and his brothers:

They served him by himself, and them by themselves, and the Egyptians who ate with him by themselves, because the Egyptians could not eat with the Hebrews, for that is an abomination to the Egyptians. (Gen. 43:32)

They could remember all of the ignominious social contrasts and recognized that the Israelites were always on the losing end, discriminated against by the Egyptians and by all those who held the upper hand. They understood that society based on productivity is always unequal:

- *Not all produce the same*, and the ones who produce more are privileged and end up with surplus value.
- *Not all own the same*, but the big producers always end up with the most property.
- *Not all consume the same*, because the ones who produce are treated with immense social entitlement.

And those who produce less and own less and consume less are devalued, devalued in the eyes of dominant society and, consequently, devalued in their own eyes. Those who produce the most and own the most and consume the most tend to be those who do not take Sabbath, even though they could. They do not take Sabbath because they are on the make . . . greedy, seeking more control, obsessed with more, because once the drive of producing, owning, and consuming becomes definitional, there is never enough yet. What an irony, those most able to keep Sabbath do not do so. And then it follows, surely, that the ones on the bottom are not permitted Sabbath. As productivity comes to obsess the haves, so the have-nots are defined by work and judged by society as lazy welfare cheats who want time off.

The interlocking relationship between the big-time producers who are mesmerized by production and the lowly workers who invisibly produce creates a social situation in which nobody is permitted Sabbath. In such an environment, defined by the practice of acquisitiveness, all parties to the social network are caught in a context of coercion that mandates always increasing production quotas, all of which echo the old imperial demand, "Make more bricks" (Exod. 5:15–19). Coercion becomes the order of the day.

All of that unbearable social reality and all of that acute social analysis are on the horizon of Moses at the Jordan. And then Moses takes a big breath, and asserts—quite unlike the words of Sinai— "Your male and female slave will be like you in their rest."

Sabbath breaks the great cycle of social contrasts and social differentiation. Sabbath rest—work stoppage—requires no expensive equipment as for polo or scuba diving or rappelling. Just stop. Just breathe. Just wait. Just rest. Just receive. Just receive life as a gift. And do so in an amazing equality, because as you look around, all manner of creatures—oxen and donkeys and livestock and zebras and pandas and oak trees and thistle and kudzu—break from the pattern of production. And now says Moses, "All manner of human creatures—landowners and slaves, urban elites and rural peasants, lords and handmaidens, ladies and eunuchs—all are invited to this exodus festival. *All rest. All break the pattern of production.* All declare, visibly and publicly, that life is not defined by meeting quotas."

IV

I could think of two instances of breaking the vicious cycles, and you may think of others:

1. In the old slave society of the South, the practice of a hoedown mattered enormously. We may think of a hoedown as down-and-dirty dancing and singing at the edge of being out of control. Well, yes, except quite likely "hoedown" meant to put down the instruments of production (in that case, to chop cotton), which are at the same time insignia of coercion. The point is not to rest in order to chop cotton better. The point rather is to create time and space precisely for the

humanness of restfulness outside the appetites of coercion that thin our humanness in fear and in fatigue.

2. A long time ago Elie Wiesel wrote a book entitled *The Jews of Silence*.[4] It concerned the oppressed Jewish community in Russia. That community lived in such fear that no member of it would even talk to Wiesel when he was in Moscow, and then one night in Moscow, Wiesel was on the street next to the Kremlin. And there were Jews dancing in the street. It was *Simchah Torah*, the festival of the Joy of the Torah. He asked a young woman who was dancing, why this exhibit of Jewish visibility in a matrix of such fear. She answered, "All year I am frightened as a Jew. Once a year, on this day, I will not be afraid. I will be a Jew and I will dance." She might have said, "I will dance like Miriam and the other women because I no longer submit to Pharaoh in Moscow."

Sabbath is the festival of egalitarianism that defies the coercion of dominant society. The first variation in the Sabbath command in Deuteronomy from Sinai is the egalitarian "like you." The second variation is the motivation for the Sabbath that has no parallel in the Sinai version:

> Remember that you were a slave in the land of Egypt, and the LORD your God brought you out from there with a mighty hand and an outstretched arm; therefore the LORD your God commanded you to keep the sabbath day. (Deut. 5:15)

It's all exodus! Because exodus is the ultimate, defining, paradigmatic work stoppage in the memory and hope of Israel. YHWH permitted work stoppage in that most demanding of empires by making clear that the workforce belongs to YHWH and not to Pharaoh. In their book *Roll Jordan Roll*, Eugene Genovese considered why slaves in the old South could get through the day without devouring insanity or hateful violence.[5] The answer suggested by their work is that every morning and night, before and after chopping cotton, the black preacher and the black mother declared with authority, "Remember, you do not belong to whitey." So Moses in Egypt, so YHWH in every coercive setting in the world:

- You do not belong to whitey;
- You do not belong to Pharaoh;

- You do not belong to Canaanite city kings;
- You do not belong to the production system.

The exodus, perhaps you noticed, permeates Deuteronomy (e.g., 6:12–14; 7:8–9; 8:12–16; 10:19; 15:15; 16:12; 24:18, 22). Everywhere exodus! Everywhere work stoppage! Everywhere end of production schedules! Everywhere end of coercion! Everywhere rest for you and peasants and slaves and beavers and carrots and the sun and moon and stars. Everywhere exodus because the exodus God is yet saturating the world with emancipation from every coercion. And we who proclaim the good news must see if the news of emancipation from coercion is the deep truth of our own lives.

End of Pharaoh's economic requirements because Pharaoh finally said to Moses:

> Then he summoned Moses and Aaron in the night, and said, "Rise up, go away from my people, both you and the Israelites! Go, worship the LORD, as you said. Take your flocks and your herds, as you said, and be gone. And bring a blessing on me too!" (Exod. 12:31–32)

End of Canaanite exploitation, as Joshua rallied around the world trade center in Jericho with its secrets and its levers of manipulation and the walls came tumbling down by peasant resistance:

> So the people shouted, and the trumpets were blown. As soon as the people heard the sound of the trumpets, they raised a great shout, and the wall fell down flat; so the people charged straight ahead into the city and captured it. (Josh. 6:20)

End of punctilious moral requirements in a graciousness that invites companionship:

> As he was setting out on a journey, a man ran up and knelt before him, and asked him, "Good Teacher, what must I do to inherit eternal life?" Jesus said to him, "Why do you call me good? No one is good but God alone. You know the commandments: 'You shall not murder; You shall not commit adultery; You shall not steal; You shall not bear false witness; You shall not defraud; Honor your father and mother.'" He said to him, "Teacher, I have kept all these since my youth." Jesus, looking at him, loved him and said, "You lack one thing; go, sell what you own, and give

the money to the poor, and you will have treasure in heaven; then come, follow me." (Mark 10:17–21)

End of excessive church expectations because it is the creation and maintenance of a zone of noncoerced well-being that is at the heart of ministry. This is what the disciples found as they traveled with Jesus, and it is what every coerced producer in our congregations most wants.

End of coercive capitalist exploitation of having to get the job with the most money because we got into the best college because we had the best SAT scores because we went to the prep school because we started at the best lower grade school because we filled our dossier with soccer and summer camp and dance lessons and church and all manner of busyness.

End of commitment to acquisitiveness that wants only commodity that dehumanizes neighbor and dehumanizes self into fatigue and resentment. Imagine, an empire—a society, a church, a family, a self—committed to productivity and shutting it all down, thereby making production penultimate, and the restful act of receptivity ultimate and defining among all the creatures.

V

This alternative offer of *restfulness*, alternative to coerciveness, does remarkable things for folk:

- It makes *art* possible, poetry, music, narratives.
- It makes *neighbor* visible, neighbor in need, neighbor in joy, neighbor in solidarity.
- It makes the *self* coherent, not divided in frantic, productive ways.
- It recognizes *God,* lover of our selves, central to the human project, not pushed aside in idolatrous pursuit of control.
- It enables us *not to worship other gods* and to violate the first three commandments.
- It makes it possible *to love neighbor* and not to covet neighbor's self.

So imagine the church as a Sabbath-keeping community that is a drastic contrast to the world of productivity. Imagine that the peasants are waiting and watching for the seventh day, and we model it. Imagine that the big-time players who are coerced by their own success also wonder if there is an alternative, and imagine that clergy as leaders are to embody and model the reality of restfulness that is rooted in God's self-giving love, this God who is a lively, life-giving alternative to every Pharaoh.

We can see in ancient Israel that they were, as alternative to Pharaoh, so drawn to Sabbath that they organized society according to what Patrick Miller terms "the sabbatic principle," an alternative to coercive acquisitiveness.[6] Moses, in the book of Deuteronomy, articulated the commandment for the year of release, a provision that the poor could not be held in hostage to the acquisitive society. In an early version of the bankruptcy law, it is proposed that poor people will have their debts canceled at the end of seven years. There is no doubt that the fix on the seventh year is an extrapolation from the Sabbath. More than that, the poor will not only have their debts canceled, but they will be given the economic wherewithal to reenter the economy with viability. In the words of Moses in Deuteronomy 15:1–18, we can tell that there was resistance to the requirement of the year of release because it could be immediately recognized that forgiveness of debts will disturb the grip of productivity. To that objection, Moses makes a characteristic plea:

> Remember that you were a slave in the land of Egypt, and the LORD your God redeemed you; for this reason I lay this command upon you today. (v. 15)

It's all about exodus! Israel will be sabbatically generous toward poor neighbors if they remember their own emancipation from coercion, if they remember they came from nowhere, and all that they have is a gift. If, however, exodus emancipation is forgotten and we imagine autonomy and self-sufficiency, then the poor person is no longer a neighbor but a competitor who is entitled to nothing. Everything depends upon remembering our own liberation to new life without brick quotas.

And, of course, after that rendition of Sabbath as generosity to the poor neighbor, Moses dreams bigger and teaches Jubilee, the readiness to give back what belongs to others after forty-nine years, the breaking of the pattern of greed (Lev. 25). In that command, Moses even precludes a charge of interest (v. 37), and then concludes:

> I am the LORD your God, who brought you out of the land of Egypt,
> to give you the land of Canaan, to be your God. (v. 38)

Moses ponders the economically dependent and then asserts that
even they belong to YHWH and not to Pharaoh:

> For they are my servants, whom I brought out of the land of Egypt;
> they shall not be sold as slaves are sold. (v. 42)

And the chapter finally concludes with yet one more exodus flourish:

> For to me the people of Israel are servants; they are my servants
> whom I brought out from the land of Egypt: I am the LORD your
> God. (v. 55)

In this threefold circle of emancipation—Sabbath, year of release,
Jubilee year—the cycle is broken! No one need any longer serve
Pharaoh or Pharaonic demand. You can run the narrative of coercion
sociologically and economically. Or you can line it out psychologically and emotionally. Or you could tell it ecclesiologically and in
terms of our vocation. It is all the same. The power of death has been
defeated! The power of life has created new life space! It is no wonder that the regime of Pharaoh shrivels and life dances. Life does not
dance at achievement or accomplishment or possession. Life dances
at gift. And that dance is the truth of our evangelical existence!

It may be imagined that such a stance on wealth and possessions
is sheer fantasy in the "real world." Such an act of imagination, however difficult and complex, continues to evoke and revivify courageous alternative imagination. Thus Sharon Ringe has shown that
the tradition of Jubilee did indeed fund gospel imagination in the
listening community around Jesus.[7] And even in our own time, the
turn of the new millennium has featured major initiatives around
Jubilee debt cancellation. It is impossible to overstate the importance
of this continuing tradition for issues of the real economy in the real
world. The tradition attests that such practices assure well-being in
the land, whereas disregard of such practices guarantees land loss.
Current attentiveness to care for the environment stands in important
continuity with the Jubilee summons. Surely the predatory economy
is causing among us "loss of land."[8] In his programmatic essay on
the history of debt, David Graeber concludes: "It seems to me that

we are long overdue for some kind of Biblical-style Jubilee; one that would affect both international debt and consumer debt."[9]

It is possible for the church to lead such a countermovement in a society that is characteristically violent and unforgiving. I have no doubt that Sabbath is the wedge that makes countercommunity of this sort viable at all, disengagement from the brutality of acquisitiveness that seeks not to take but to give as the creator God has given life. If the church is to be such an alternative, then its leadership must model that alternative life, not in conspicuous performance, but in lives genuinely at rest. This alternative is choosable. Our mothers and fathers had to choose to leave Pharaoh's Egypt. The invitation to follow is always a choice, to follow the Lord of the Sabbath. It is news and practice and possibility for which the world desperately waits. Imagine all of us, men and women, boys and girls, oxen and donkeys and radishes and porcupines and sun and moon and stars . . . all at rest, all forgiven, all at Sabbath . . . just like us!

Questions for Reflection

1. Wealth and possessions are a part of our everyday lives. Israel is instructed that their use of wealth should be bound up in the needs of the neighbor. Does your core confession of wealth center on neighborliness, just as Israel's did?

2. As we ponder the stories of gold in Exodus, consider how stories about possessions manifest in your life. How are you setting your wealth in a narrative of deep anxiety and self-securing? How are you setting your wealth in a narrative of generous gratitude and expectation?

3. The Sabbath calls us to stop, rest, and breathe. This work stoppage breaks the cycles and systems of social differentiation by equalizing all people. Can you really stop working? Do you think society is capable of work stoppage? What might the world look like if all of us stopped, rested, and breathed?

4. Brueggemann asserts that the year of release, the year of Jubilee, is indeed a possibility, something that the church can choose. Take some time to draw, creatively write about, or ponder what a year of Jubilee would look like for you and your neighbors.

Chapter 7

Neighborly Compassion in the Book of Deuteronomy

The community of Israel, now bound in covenant to YHWH and now committed to Sabbath, lingered at Sinai where, as we have seen, Israel made a defining choice. It decided to trust the God who made heaven and earth (Exod. 20:11), to rely on the guaranteed reliabilities of the creation, and to eschew the anxiety that comes from loss of confidence in the sureness of the creator and the goodness of creation. That defining choice, however, was not easy to sustain.

I

The oath of allegiance to YHWH is sworn in Exodus 24. But by Exodus 32, when Moses had been gone from them for forty days and nights (see 24:18), the God of the covenant seemed remote, and they fell back to anxiety. The God who was their guarantor against anxiety seemed absent.

And so they acted in their acute anxiety. They gathered their gold (what else?), their precious earrings, their most treasured, coveted commodity, and they made their own god. They imagined that with a rightly honored commodity they could "purchase" security in a world that seemed devoid of the creator. "God-making" amid anxiety is a standard human procedure!

But of course, such god-making of ersatz gods evoked great anger on the part of the creator of heaven and earth. As a consequence of such anxious behavior, Moses broke the tablets of Sinai, and the covenant was dissolved. Israel was for an instant hopeless, and Moses was

93

bereft. In Exodus 32–34, Moses bargained with YHWH, prayed, and postured. In response to Moses' insistence, the God who nullified the covenant committed an enormous act of forgiveness. Even beyond Israel's disobedient anxiety, YHWH was prepared to begin again:

> He said: I hereby make a covenant. Before all your people I will perform marvels, such as have not been performed in all the earth or in any nation; and all the people among whom you live shall see the work of the LORD; for it is an awesome thing that I will do with you. (Exod. 34:10)

Then, with the broken covenant restored, in Numbers 10:11, Israel left Sinai on its way to the land of promise.

After forty years, they arrived at the Jordan, at the very edge of the land promised to Abraham and Sarah. They were ready to leap the Jordan to get there, these land-hungry peasants, ready to swim the Jordan, these land-desperate desert people. But then they stopped at the Jordan River. They stopped there longer than they intended because Moses had final instructions, long final instructions that we call the book of Deuteronomy.

As we have seen, the exodus story tells the fundamental biblical narrative of salvation. And yet, beginning already in the wilderness on the way to the mountain and continuing in their anxiety as Moses lingered on the mountain, it turns out that the exodus memory, whatever may be its historical rootage, became a paradigmatic narrative through which all social reality is described and reexperienced.[1] That is, the narrative pertains to a onetime remembered social upheaval caused by God's holiness; but the narrative looks beyond that memory to see that the same transactions of oppression and emancipation continue everywhere to evoke holy power. The exodus narrative concerns the passion of *holy power* in response to *human cry*.[2] Israel is always in the context of cry, and always departing from such context. The narrative moves out beyond Israel to see that this is the narrative quality of the entire human historical process.[3]

In the Old Testament, it remained for the tradition of Deuteronomy to codify and institutionalize that narrative memory of the exodus in order to make it a charter for ordering society.[4] The book of Deuteronomy classically transposes the particular *memory* in the narrative into a set of *commandments* mandating that the radical neighborliness exhibited by YHWH in the exodus as an alternative to Pharaoh should become the organizing principle of Israel's life in the new land.

II

In the text, the land is said to be the "land of the Canaanites," and Moses speaks so long to the Israelites because he regards the move into the new land as a high-risk venture. He wants to be sure that Israel understands that the old, desert covenant still pertains to the agricultural territory they are about to enter, a land that is claimed as well by other gods who are inimical to YHWH. Moses regards the land of Canaan, it being so fertile, as an enormous temptation and a huge seduction to Israel. Moses knows that the affluence of the land is sure to create a crisis in covenant faith.

We cannot understand the crisis of land in that tradition unless we understand what Moses means by "Canaanites." It turns out that "Canaanite" is not an ethnic term. It is likely that those called "Canaanite" are ethnically identical to those who became Israelites. The differences are not ethnic but political, economic, sociological, and eventually theological. The term "Canaanite" comes from the term "purple," and refers first of all to those who traded in purple dyes. Then the term comes to refer to all those who engaged in commerce who operated a money economy, as distinct from peasants and nomads, pastoral and agricultural people. Eventually the term "Canaanite" comes to refer to those who have mastered the urban economy, built cities as centers of military and political power, and developed the sociological patterns that belong to urban life—social stratification, division of labor, and surplus value.[5] Moses, good sociologist that he was, was able to see that such complex social relationships that are generically labeled "Canaanite" are inimical to the covenant community with its passion for more or less egalitarian or communitarian relationships. Thus the Moses tradition—then extended by Elijah—is that there is a clash of social systems that is reflective of a clash of theological passions.[6]

Moses pauses at the Jordan River to instruct the covenant community that is pledged to egalitarianism, because he knows that the land under "Canaanite" aegis is enormously seductive to Israel, and its seduction constitutes a threat to covenantal models of social relationships. In response to that anticipated seduction and threat, Moses offers several homiletical pieces, of which I cite four:

- In Deuteronomy 6, Moses warns that the advanced, affluent standard of living in Canaanite culture would produce amnesia in Israel about the past and indifference to the God of the exodus:

  > When the LORD your God has brought you into the land that he swore to your ancestors, to Abraham, to Isaac, and to Jacob, to give you—a land with fine, large cities that you did not build, houses filled with all sorts of goods that you did not fill, hewn cisterns that you did not hew, vineyards and olive groves that you did not plant—and when you have eaten your fill, *take care that you do not forget the LORD*, who brought you out of the land of Egypt, out of the house of slavery. The LORD your God you shall fear; him you shall serve, and by his name alone you shall swear. Do not follow other gods, any of the gods of the peoples who are all around you, because the LORD your God, who is present with you, is a jealous God. The anger of the LORD your God would be kindled against you and he would destroy you from the face of the earth. (vv. 10–15, emphasis added)

  This warning about "other gods," as is characteristic in Israel, is inescapable. The contract is at the same time a warning about other systems of social relationships that are inimical to YHWH.

- In Deuteronomy 7, Moses reminds Israel that its peculiar identity is a gift from YHWH, and maintenance of that identity is urgent:

  > For you are a people holy to the LORD your God; the LORD your God has chosen you out of all the peoples on earth to be his people, his treasured possession.
  > It was not because you were more numerous than any other people that the LORD set his heart on you and chose you—for you were the fewest of all peoples. It was because the LORD loved you and kept the oath that he swore to your ancestors, that the LORD has brought

you out with a mighty hand, and redeemed you from the house of slavery, from the hand of Pharaoh king of Egypt. (vv. 6–8)

That distinctiveness, moreover, required purgation of all advertising slogans and icons of the Canaanite social system that would seduce or challenge:

But this is how you must deal with them: break down their altars, smash their pillars, hew down their sacred poles, and burn their idols with fire. (v. 5)

- In Deuteronomy 8, the best known of these reflections, Moses is back to the danger of amnesia due to affluence:

For the Lord your God is bringing you into a good land, a land with flowing streams, with springs and underground waters welling up in valleys and hills, a land of wheat and barley, of vines and fig trees and pomegranates, a land of olive trees and honey, a land where you may eat bread without scarcity, where you will lack nothing, a land whose stones are iron and from whose hills you may mine copper. You shall eat your fill and bless the Lord your God for the good land that he has given you.

Take care that you do not forget the Lord your God, by failing to keep his commandments, his ordinances, and his statutes, which I am commanding you today. When you have eaten your fill and have built fine houses and live in them, and when your herds and flocks have multiplied, and your silver and gold is multiplied, and all that you have is multiplied, *then do not exalt yourself, forgetting the Lord your God,* who brought you out of the land of Egypt, out of the house of slavery, who led you through the great and terrible wilderness, an arid wasteland with poisonous snakes and scorpions. He made water flow for you from flint rock, and fed you in the wilderness with manna that your ancestors did not know, to humble you and to test you, and in the end to do you good. Do not say to yourself, "My power and the might of my own hand have gotten me this wealth." But remember the Lord your God, for it is he who gives you power to get wealth, so that he may confirm his covenant that he swore to your ancestors, as he is doing today. (vv. 7–18, emphasis added)

Amnesia will cause Israelites to sign on to Canaanite perceptions of reality. Israel will forget that its life is a gift of the generous Creator and a miracle accomplished by a powerful redeemer; Israel will imagine it is autonomous and without accountability. And says Moses, "If you imagine that long enough, the covenantal option of neighborliness will disappear, and all will become Canaanites":

If you do forget the LORD your God and follow other gods to serve and worship them, I solemnly warn you today that you shall surely perish. Like the nations that the LORD is destroying before you, so shall you perish, because you would not obey the voice of the LORD your God. (vv. 19–20)

- Finally, in Deuteronomy 10:12–22, Moses reflects on the God who is full of grace and truth. We have beheld his glory:

    For the LORD your God is God of gods and Lord of lords, the great God, mighty and awesome, . . . (v. 17a)

But that glory is evidenced in graciousness:

. . . who is not partial and takes no bribe, who executes justice for the orphan and the widow, and who loves the strangers, providing them food and clothing. (vv. 17b–18)

With a recall to the exodus and the wonder of liberation from the Pharaonic system of brick quotas, Israel as alternative community is empowered to neighborly compassion:

You shall also love the stranger, for you were strangers in the land of Egypt. You shall fear the LORD your God; him alone you shall worship; to him you shall hold fast, and by his name you shall swear. (vv. 19–20)

The urging of Moses is that the radical neighborliness exhibited by YHWH in the exodus as an alternative to Pharaoh should become the organizing principle of Israel's life in the new land. The alternative of YHWH to Pharaoh is to organize a society resistant to Canaanite seduction, and the pivot point of it all is neighborliness, for neither

Pharaoh in Egypt nor the Canaanites has a clue about the neighbor. "Canaanites" characteristically viewed the other as commodity, as threat, as rival, as competitor. It is only YHWH, the God of neighborliness, who breaks the cycle of commodity pressure for the sake of the neighborhood. And as we have seen, Sabbath is a decisive gesture in the breaking of that cycle. The seduction of the land is that Israelites would join the "Canaanite" enterprise, that is, the pursuit of commodity, the commitment to productivity, and the consequent inevitable erosion of the neighborly commitments of Sinai.

III

But Moses at the Jordan River not only issues a warning. He also, in quite concrete ways, envisions that the "land of Canaan," the society given over to commodity and productivity and antineighborly ways, can be transformed. That is, market relations can be radically transposed into neighborly relations by a different set of neighborly practices. Indeed the "legal corpus" of Deuteronomy—half commandment and half sermonic appeal—is committed to alternative social relationships. In quite concrete ways, Israel is a "countersociety" that is in contrast to the remembered political economy of Pharaoh and the experienced political economy of Canaanite city-states:

- Moses proposed dismantling the economic arrangement of slavery by permitting village protection for runaway slaves:

  Slaves who have escaped to you from their owners shall not be given back to them. They shall reside with you, in your midst, in any place they choose in any one of your towns, wherever they please; you shall not oppress them. (23:15–16)

- Moses seeks to protect the covenantal economy by prohibiting usury within the neighborly community, a practice much sanctioned belatedly in the Calvinist tradition:

  You shall not charge interest on loans to another Israelite, interest on money, interest on provisions, interest on anything that is lent. On loans to a foreigner you may charge interest, but on loans to another Israelite you may not charge interest, so that the LORD your God may bless you in all your undertakings in the land that you are about to enter and possess. (vv. 19–20)

Verse 19 uses the term "interest" five times as a verb and a noun. The tradition knows, as vulnerable people always discover, that charging interest is an enormous leverage that moneyed forces use against unmoneyed people to reduce them to dependency that becomes a form of slavery. The distinctiveness of Israel shows up exactly in such a prohibition of economic exploitation of the vulnerable. The regulation connects this economic no-no with the well-being of the land. The earlier regulation of Exodus 22:25 identifies the "poor" as the subject of the commandment, an intent implicit here as well.

- Moses prohibits taking as loan insurance the "means of production" from a worker that would deny the capacity to earn a living:

   No one shall take a mill or an upper millstone in pledge, for that would be taking a life in pledge. (Deut. 24:6)

- Moses prohibits forcing anyone into economic bondage and reduction to slavery:

   If someone is caught kidnaping another Israelite, enslaving or selling the Israelite, then that kidnaper shall die. So you shall purge the evil from your midst. (v. 7)

- Moses prohibits excessive collateral for a loan from a poor person, urging instead a regularly repeated neighborly gesture:

   When you make your neighbor a loan of any kind, you shall not go into the house to take the pledge. You shall wait outside, while the person to whom you are making the loan brings the pledge out to you. If the person is poor, you shall not sleep in the garment given you as the pledge. You shall give the pledge back by sunset, so that your neighbor may sleep in the cloak and bless you; and it will be to your credit before the LORD your God. (vv. 10–13)

The initial prohibition concerns the process of receiving collateral ("pledge") from a neighbor (vv. 10–11). But verse

12 moves attention yet again to the poor, the ones without protection or resources in economic matters. The regulation provides that a "garment" (coat) taken as collateral can be kept only during the day, because the poor person will need it at night to keep warm. The daytime collateral returned at night offers the ludicrous picture of each day claiming collateral and every night returning it to the debtor. Imagine doing that each day and each night for a thirty-year loan! Surely the intent is to make collateral so inconvenient that it is not demanded in the first place.

- Moses prohibits the practice of withholding pay from poor laborers, of saying that "the check is in the mail":

> You shall not withhold the wages of poor and needy laborers, whether other Israelites or aliens who reside in your land in one of your towns. You shall pay them their wages daily before sunset, because they are poor and their livelihood depends on them; otherwise they might cry to the LORD against you, and you would incur guilt. (vv. 14–15)

The tradition knows that withholding wages, even for a day, permits the use of money by the employed that rightly belongs to the laborers. Of course beyond that, there are now, as surely then, many forms of wage theft. The failure to pay on the day earned is not simply antineighborly. It will evoke a cry to YHWH, not unlike the initial cry of Israel to YHWH in Egypt (Exod. 2:23–25). That cry will cause YHWH to hold the exploiter to account. It is worth noting that in this regulation, as in Deuteronomy 24:10–14, the limit of antineighborly collateral or withheld wages must end at "sunset." It is as though economic leverage is permitted (collateral and withholding wages), but at sunset in the rhythm of creation, all such leverage must cease in the practice of neighborliness (see Ps. 104:21–23). Economic leverage has severe limitations that are ordered in the rhythm of creation that cannot be safely disregarded.

- Moses focuses upon the characteristically poor and vulnerable in the community, those at the low end of influence and leverage, most vulnerable to exploitation in the world of capital and labor:

> You shall not deprive a *resident alien* or an *orphan* of justice; you shall not take a *widow's* garment in pledge. Remember that you were a slave in Egypt and the LORD your God redeemed you from there; therefore I command you to do this. (Deut. 24:17–18, emphasis added)

Verse 17 broadens the target group of limitation on collateral stipulated in verses 10–13 from "your neighbor" to include orphans, widows, and immigrants as well. Verse 18 gives motivation for this limitation on collateral with reference to the exodus deliverance. Exploitative collateral is reminiscent of Pharaoh's rapacious economics, and it must be shunned in the alternative economy of Israel.

• Whereas the preceding regulations concerning interest, collateral, and withholding wages were designed to restrain exploitation, here Moses commends positive action toward the vulnerable by urging that welfare provisions in an agricultural economy must be provided:

> When you reap your harvest in your field and forget a sheaf in the field, you shall not go back to get it; it shall be left for the *alien*, the *orphan*, and the *widow*, so that the LORD your God may bless you in all your undertakings. When you beat your olive trees, do not strip what is left; it shall be for the *alien*, the *orphan*, and the *widow*.
> When you gather the grapes of your vineyard, do not glean what is left; it shall be for the *alien*, the *orphan*, and the *widow*. Remember that you were a slave in the land of Egypt; therefore I am commanding you to do this. (vv. 19–22, emphasis added)

The threefold provision concerning grain (harvest), olive (oil), and grapes (for wine) concerns the familiar triad of money crops. Because these are money crops with potentially large commercial profit, one might expect that the growers would be sure to extract every possible measure of them.

But not in Israel! In Israel, unlike the "Canaanite" economy of squeezed commodities, these money crops must be managed in a neighborly way.[7] When the provision goes on to identify the neighbors, it reiterates the triad of the vul nerable—widows, orphans, immigrants—those without resources or legal protections in a patriarchal society. For good reason, Frank Crüsemann has termed this provision an early "social safety net" in which agriculture for profit is curbed by the presence and need of the neighbor. He concludes:

> This whole inter-coordinated system of laws for social security springs from a fundamental deuteronomic idea: the freedom that has been experienced, which exodus and land represent and which is manifest in the freedom of the agricultural population, includes freedom from requirements of payment of tribute or compulsory labor (to the state). It is limited only by the double connection to the giver of freedom and to those who do not participate in freedom to the same degree. Guarantees of social security and survival are established for all problem groups and those [who] might be threatened. Furthermore, this relationship is not portrayed as a moral appeal for charity, but as law. Only by passing on this freedom and wealth can the continuance of these gifts be secured.[8]

In a predatory economy, the great anxiety is that someone will get something for nothing. The assumption of such a mantra is the privatization of wealth and the autonomy of the owner of such produce. This regulation, however, refuses such privatization and insists that such productive wealth has a social public dimension. Thus the law is a break with conventional privatized economics; that break, moreover, is specified by yet another reference to the exodus in verse 22. The sum of all of these regulations is the assurance that the emancipatory actions of the exodus remain in the work of the economy.

- Moses provides "cities of refuge" for accidental death, perhaps an easement against capital punishment:

> Now this is the case of a homicide who might flee there and live, that is, someone who has killed another person unintentionally when the two had not been at enmity before: Suppose someone goes into the forest with another to cut wood, and when one of them swings the ax to cut

down a tree, the head slips from the handle and strikes the
other person who then dies; the killer may flee to one of
these cities and live. But if the distance is too great, the
avenger of blood in hot anger might pursue and overtake
and put the killer to death, although a death sentence was
not deserved, since the two had not been at enmity before.
Therefore I command you: You shall set apart three cities. (19:4–7)

• Moses limits corporal punishment in the interest of not humiliat-
ing the subject of punishment:

Suppose two persons have a dispute and enter into litiga-
tion, and the judges decide between them, declaring one
to be in the right and the other to be in the wrong. If the
one in the wrong deserves to be flogged, the judge shall
make that person lie down and be beaten in his presence
with the number of lashes proportionate to the offense.
Forty lashes may be given but not more; if more lashes
than these are given, your neighbor will be degraded in
your sight. (25:1–3)

• Moses provides honest trade provisions, so that the poor are not
exploited:

You shall not have in your bag two kinds of weights,
large and small. You shall not have in your house two
kinds of measures, large and small. You shall have only
a full and honest weight; you shall have only a full and
honest measure, so that your days may be long in the land
that the LORD your God is giving you. For all who do such
things, all who act dishonestly, are abhorrent to the LORD
your God. (vv. 13–16)

Here the concluding regulation of the legal corpus of Deuteronomy concerns exploitative commercial practices specified by "two kinds of weights" and "two kinds of measures."
Such practices give traders, merchants, and bankers enormous discretion about which weight or measure to use with
which client. It may be readily inferred that one measure or
weight would be utilized for one's friends, and another for
the less-favored neighbors. It takes no imagination to trans-

fer this regulation to our contemporary practice of exploitative interest rates and payday loans for the disadvantaged,
or no-bid contracts for the well-connected. Thus the provision insists upon social equity of an egalitarian kind, so that
the privileged, entitled, and advantaged do not receive, as in
a predatory economy, still further advantage. This regulation is reflected in the indictment of Amos 8:5–6, in which
"deceit" is practiced against the poor and needy with exor-
bitant price arrangements. The Torah was a great protector
against the toxic temptations of a predatory economy.

Now, of course, these laws are quite concrete and designed for
a simple, face-to-face agricultural community. The sum of them,
however, is a vision of a radically alternative society in which
neighborly commitments supersede all the requirements of commodity production and consumption. The news is that "Canaanite"
society and its pattern of exploitative relationships can end, can
be transformed into covenantal relationships that concern not only
interpersonal interactions, but also institutional practices and policy
commitments.

IV

These two accent points, I believe, summarize the urgency of Moses
at the Jordan River:

1. *The land is seductive* because it is organized in "Canaanite"
ways that preclude serious neighborly interaction.

2. *The land is transformable*; that transformation is accomplished
by daily concrete attentiveness to neighborly interaction that is not to
be defined by the market. That is, Israelites are not to act in "Canaanite" ways, but in ways that derive from the passions of Sinai. Indeed,
if Israel were to persist in "Canaanite" ways, to which it is susceptible
in its amnesia, it will undo the covenant at Sinai. Eventually it will
undo the emancipation from Egypt, and will find itself back in the grip
of Pharaonic slavery. For in fact what the tradition of Deuteronomy
terms "Canaanite" is in the end a replication of Pharaonic slavery.
The consequence is that Israel must always again, in every circumstance, always again, leave Egypt and commit to an alternative.

The dynamism of the book of Deuteronomy keeps the vision of an alternative society richly available. The book of Deuteronomy itself understands that the teaching of Moses is not an old, fixed, settled point, but is always a reiteration that is done with imaginative freedom in order to be pertinent to a new form of the issues of acquisitiveness versus neighborliness.

Questions for Reflection

1. In our anxious times and in the midst of our own anxiety, we tend to play the game of "god-making" so that we may purchase security for ourselves. Do you find yourself leaning into "god-making"? What types of "gods" are you creating in order to make yourself secure?

2. Moses urged the Israelites to remember their relationship with YHWH and with one another, to never forget and thus fall into the systems of the Canaanites. As you move through life trying to respond to God's call of neighborliness, are you experiencing a state of amnesia, forgetting the call of God? What has caused you to forget?

3. The covenant laid out in Deuteronomy highlights the economic and financial matters of the time, which are similar to our own—involving predatory interest rates, wage withholding, and placing profit over employee. Take a look at your local context (businesses, laws, finance, agriculture, etc.). In what ways are these entities or systems exploiting those who are experiencing poverty, the orphan, the widow, and the immigrant?

4. Taking into account what you notice in your local context, what are practical and tangible ways you can help to transform these systems into relationships of neighborliness? What limits are there on the things that you can do personally to redress these systems? What systemic solutions to these systemic problems can you imagine, and how might you advocate for them in your context?

Chapter 8

The Dynamism of the Deuteronomic Tradition

*T*he previous chapter shows how Deuteronomy transforms the emancipation from Egypt from a memory of a past event into the organizing principle for Israel's ongoing social reality, a reality that remains constantly vulnerable to being forgotten in an affluent environment. That is, the *emancipatory instructions* in the book of Deuteronomy are grounded in the *emancipatory imagination* that engages the story and teachings of Moses not as settled historical events, but as open to new iterations in the ongoing contest between rival socioeconomic systems of acquisitiveness versus neighborliness. This chapter continues to explore the dynamic, emancipatory imagination of the Deuteronomic tradition.

Of course, my interest in this dynamic contest is not antiquarian. There is also a contest of narratives going on in our society that is urgent, passionate, and sometimes mean-spirited. In this contest the world can be rendered in very different ways that yield very different assurances and very different requirements. It is a very old contest, already formed and articulated in ancient Israel, a contest in which that ancient community found no settled resolution. It is also a quite contemporary contest, one in which the shape of our society is at stake and the character and conduct of the church is at stake. And because we tend to be preoccupied with immediately pressing issues, we tend not to notice or linger over the narrative milieu in which immediate issues are situated and by which they are defined. Here I propose to trace this contest of narratives through some biblical texts, and to reflect on the demanding contemporaneity of that ancient exercise.

I

In the book of Deuteronomy, the issue of acquisitiveness versus neighborliness is set in the thirteenth century BCE, just at the Jordan River, at the edge of Canaan. The primal memory of the Bible is that Israel represents an alternative to Canaan. In critical study, however, the Mosaic placement of Deuteronomy is taken to be a fictive construct. It is conventional to date the appearance of Deuteronomy in the eighth and seventh centuries BCE, perhaps under the influence of Near Eastern covenant-treaty formulations. In that context, Deuteronomy stands at the headwaters of the "classical prophets" of the eighth and seventh centuries, with their urgent accent on covenantalism. This linkage pertains especially to the prophetic traditions of Hosea and Jeremiah, which are intimately related to Deuteronomy, but more broadly it relates to the entire corpus of prophetic speeches of judgment. In that context, it is recognized that Israel has gone amiss if not completely failed in its covenantal mandate under the impetus of the Jerusalem religious–economic elites. Thus Deuteronomy is a summons to return to covenantal practices, including economic neighborliness. Insofar as Israel has fallen into predatory economics, it has placed its life in the land in jeopardy. If we imagine some version of Deuteronomy during the reign of Josiah, the book urges the Israelites not to give in to Assyrian definitions of reality as King Ahaz so readily did in 2 Kings 16.

But more recent critical study of the Old Testament is inclined to locate Deuteronomy not in the seventh but rather in the fifth century BCE, in the period of Persian domination. If placed there, it is in the wake of the loss of land and political independence, so that Judah has been reduced to a Persian province, and the elite, upon return to the land, remain under Persian control. In that context, Deuteronomy serves as a prospective guide for how to order the life and economy of Israel upon return to and recovery of the land of promise. Because life under Persia is experienced as "slavery" (in the form of taxation; see Ezra 9:8; Neh. 9:36), the reordering of the economy is urgent. Deuteronomy thus may be a document peculiarly suited to the reforms of Ezra and Nehemiah. Nehemiah's remarkable action in Nehemiah 5 has the fingerprints of Deuteronomy all over it. In that narrative account, rich Jews are taxing poor Jews to death.

And there were those who said, "We are having to borrow money on our fields and vineyards to pay the king's tax. Now our flesh is the same as that of our kindred; our children are the same as their children; and yet we are forcing our sons and daughters to be slaves, and some of our daughters have been ravished; we are powerless, and our fields and vineyards now belong to others." (5:4–5)

Nehemiah responds to that exploitative economic transaction with powerful indignation:

I was very angry when I heard their outcry and these complaints. After thinking it over, I brought charges against the nobles and the officials; I said to them, "You are all taking interest from your own people." And I called a great assembly to deal with them. (vv. 6–7)

And then, reformer that he is, Nehemiah proposes restorative action:

Moreover I and my brothers and my servants are lending them money and grain. Let us stop this taking of interest. Restore to them, this very day, their fields, their vineyards, their olive orchards, and their houses, and the interest on money, grain, wine, and oil that you have been exacting from them. Then they said, "We will restore everything and demand nothing more from them. We will do as you say." And I called the priests, and made them take an oath to do as they had promised. (vv. 10–12)

This is a clear example of the way in which covenantal solidarity outflanks the raw power of economic transaction. Nehemiah's actions are in sync with Moses in Deuteronomy, and clearly reflect elemental Sinai commitments.

Thus the teaching of Deuteronomy pertains (a) to the thirteenth-century-BCE canonical context at the edge of the land of promise, (b) to the eighth and seventh centuries when Israel is jeopardized by compromise, (c) to the fifth century in the Persian period, when Israel ponders a restored community, (d) or to *any* century.

Moreover, Deuteronomy is quite self-conscious in seeing that the issue of acquisitiveness practiced in amnesia versus neighborliness practiced in vigorous memory is everywhere a recurring issue. For that reason Deuteronomy is fundamentally a process of dynamic interpretation, always connecting the primal issues to the circumstance of the day.

- Thus, the narrative reports:

  > Beyond the Jordan in the land of Moab, Moses undertook
  > to expound this law as follows. (Deut. 1:5)

  The term "expound" is tricky, but clearly Moses did not
  merely reiterate the Torah of Sinai. Rather he interpreted it,
  thus making a stark covenantal ethic pertinent to an agricultural economy.

- In 5:2–3, Moses asserts that the covenant which invites to an
  alternative society is not a one-time deal, but must always be
  articulated afresh:

  > The LORD our God made a covenant with us at Horeb.
  > Not with our ancestors did the LORD make this covenant,
  > but with us, who are all of us here alive today.

  Moses remembers the ancient covenant of Sinai (Horeb)
  made to a previous generation in Israel. But then, in a series
  of words that Moses piles up—"all of us, here, alive, this
  day"—the covenant is said to be immediately contemporary for the new generation. This is the core argument of
  the book of Deuteronomy, the center of covenantal teaching in the Bible. The economy is not a rat race in which
  people remain exhausted from coercive goals; it is, rather,
  a covenantal enterprise for the sake of the whole community. Even in a new circumstance of agricultural possibility,
  the old desert covenant is defining. Moses expects Israel to
  reject the acquisitive culture of its neighbors for the sake of
  a covenantal alternative. It must be done again in the seventh
  century, in the fifth century, in the time of Jesus, who rein-
  terprets Torah, and now, in our own time and place.

- That process of reinterpretation, further, is indicated in 17:18,
  where it is said, according to the usual rendering,

  > [w]hen he has taken the throne of his kingdom, he shall
  > have a copy of this law written for him in the presence of
  > the levitical priests.

  In Greek, the term "copy" is *deuteros*, from which comes
  the name "Deuteronomy." But perhaps the term means "second" and thus "second edition" of the Torah, that is, not the

Torah at Sinai, but now Torah in an agricultural community with a threat and a challenge to Canaanite acquisitiveness that was hardly on the screen at Sinai. In fact, Deuteronomy is a model for always producing "new versions" of Torah, and indeed, Jesus himself in his formulation, "You have heard it said of old, . . . But I say to you," offers a new version of Torah that matters to the present crisis (see Matt. 5:21, 27, 31, 33, 38, 43).

These hints of dynamism in Deuteronomy 1:5, 5:3, and 17:18 are given fuller exhibit in the work of Ezra, the primal scribal teacher of Judaism. In the founding moment of Judaism, it is said that as the assembly listened, the reading Levites

helped the people to understand the law, while the people remained in their places. So they read from the book, from the law of God, with interpretation. They gave the sense, so that the people understood the reading. (Neh. 8:7–8)

The task of authorizing, empowering, and envisioning a community of neighborly practice as an alternative to acquisitiveness is an unending task in which we ourselves are engaged.

II

We may now add a third premise to the two established in the previous chapter's exploration of Deuteronomy:

1. The land of acquisitiveness is seductive to those who are victims of amnesia.

2. The land of acquisitiveness is transformable into a land of neighborliness.

3. The interpretive process is a dynamic one whereby the contest of acquisitiveness versus neighborliness, Canaanite versus Israelite, life versus death, is a constant that takes many variable forms. We may see that defining issue given classic articulation in the hardnosed summary of Moses:

See, I have set before you today life and prosperity, death and adversity. If you obey the commandments of the LORD your God that I am commanding you today, by loving the LORD your God, walking in his ways, and observing his commandments, decrees, and ordinances, then you shall live and become numerous, and the Lord your God will bless you in the land that you are entering to possess. But if your heart turns away and you do not hear, but are led astray to bow down to other gods and serve them, I declare to you today that you shall perish; you shall not live long in the land that you are crossing the Jordan to enter and possess. I call heaven and earth to witness against you today that I have set before you life and death, blessings and curses. Choose life so that you and your descendants may live, loving the Lord your God, obeying him, and holding fast to him; for that means life to you and length of days, so that you may live in the land that the Lord swore to give to your ancestors, to Abraham, to Isaac, and to Jacob. (Deut. 30:15–20)

The *either* of "life and prosperity" concerns adherence to the Torah, which in context means the Torah of Deuteronomy. Thus the commandments of Deuteronomy are presented as prerequisite for life and the land, and many of these commandments concern wealth and possessions. The *or* of "death and adversity" is to compromise or abandon the covenantal distinctiveness of Israel and to conform to the regnant predatory economy. The either-or of Deuteronomy is, of course, cast as a religious issue of true God or false gods; attention to the text, however, makes clear that *religious claims* are deeply intertwined with *socioeconomic issues*, so that the decision of life or death before Israel (in any of these contexts) is a decision that concerns wealth and possessions. The move in the tradition from religious criticism to economic criticism anticipates the aphorism of Karl Marx:

> The criticism of heaven is thus transformed into the criticism
>   of earth,
> The criticism of religion into the criticism of law, and
> The criticism of theology into the criticism of politics.[1]

Thus a warning against *false religion* in Deuteronomy entails a warning against *false economic practice*. The rhetoric of Deuteronomy is focused on the command to "love the Lord your God with all your heart" (6:5); this mandate, however, is accompanied by the tacit commandment to "love your neighbor" (Lev. 19:18), so that the either-or that concerns God also concerns wealth and possessions in a decision for or against neighborliness in economic policy and practice. A neighborly economy must be at the heart of any biblical understanding of salvation.

The accent on a neighborly economy is pervasive in the corpus and is in no sense confined to a particular set of commandments. The overall aim of the commandments is to subordinate the economy to the requirements of neighborly society, so that debt and its economic leverage over the vulnerable are not defining for social relationships. We may identify four texts that concern *offerings* through which material possessions are to be shared with the community of the vulnerable. The tithe is a specified amount of produce that is owed in an agricultural community to the landowner. Thus a tithe brought to YHWH's sanctuary is an acknowledgment that YHWH is the landowner, and not the one who occupies the land (see Ps. 24:1). In Deuteronomy 14:22–29 there are three provisions for the tithe:

- The tithe of grain, wine, olive oil, herds, and flocks (all the best agricultural produce) is to be eaten by the donor in the presence of "the LORD your God," that is, at the sanctuary. This is a curious provision; no doubt the requirement is that the donor will, by such eating, acknowledge the sovereignty of God, who gives the produce. It is like being welcomed at a table to eat, all the while recognizing that the table belongs to another. The act is a gesture against any imagined autonomy by acknowledgment of YHWH as the producer of the crops and provider at the table.
- If the distance to the sanctuary is great, the produce can be cashed out for "silver." The regulation makes clear that this is a required economic transaction that is not to be taken too romantically. The money is for whatever one wants, but in the presence of YHWH.
- In the third year, the tithe is offered not at the sanctuary but in the village, to be shared with the vulnerable: immigrants, orphans, widows, and also Levites. The purpose is to sustain those without resources, an act that will evoke God's blessing. All three of these actions tell against any notion that the tithe (owed money) is "mine." The tithe asserts YHWH's rule over Israel and over the land.

In the festival calendar of Deuteronomy 16, two of the three festivals are a vehicle for providing generous sustenance for the stranger. In the Festival of Weeks, the guest list is inclusive: "Rejoice before the LORD your God—you and your sons and your daughters, your male and female slaves, the Levites resident in your towns, as well as the strangers, the orphans, and the widows who are among you" (vv. 11–12).

In the Festival of Booths, there is a parallel inclusiveness (v. 14). In the summary statement, moreover, participation in the festivals to YHWH requires that one not be "empty-handed" (v. 16). The worshiper must bring a substantive offering, an act that attests the materiality of Israel's faith and that precludes any misunderstanding of Israel's worship as a spiritual act detached from questions of money and possessions and their faithful management. In the provision for Passover, the festival is securely placed in the narrative of the exodus. The unleavened bread, the bread of affliction, is a remembrance, "because you came out of the land of Egypt in great haste, so that all the days of your life you may remember the day of your departure from the land of Egypt" (v. 3).

In verse 12, moreover, the motivation for a generous offering is the exodus. Either directly or by implication, all of these festival celebrations draw Israel back into its narrative of emancipation, in order to affirm that Israel's life, identity, and destiny are outside the domain of the coercive economy. The question of who has access to the produce of the community is an acute one. Here the answer is that all members of the community have access, enough to rejoice together and to be sated.

III

The accent of Deuteronomy's either-or, however, is not preoccupied with cultic matters. It is focused on civic, social regulations that will keep covenantal life viable. This accent is in contrast to the priestly tradition of Leviticus, which is largely preoccupied with cultic questions. Most important of all of these civic, social provisions is the regulation on debt in the Year of Release, that is, "remission of debts" in the seventh year.[2] The core regulation in 15:1 is terse and unqualified. It is a simple, defining recognition that debt does not have an ultimate role to play in the economy and that the community has a profound stake in the management of debt so that it does not become defining for the community. This is a remarkable provision that lies at the heart of forgiveness in biblical faith. As Patrick Miller has shown with reference to a text in Luke, forgiveness was primarily an economic matter before it became a theological agenda.[3] (It is with reference to that fact that some versions of the Lord's Prayer concern forgiveness of "debts.")

At the outset we may acknowledge the ever-recurring question of whether, in fact, such a practice was implemented in Israel. It is telling, indeed, that of all the requirements in the ancient Torah, it is this one that evokes such wonderment. Such anxious wonderment is recognition of how peculiar and dangerous such a provision would be to the maintenance of an ordinary economy. My sense about such a question is that it is characteristically a desire to be reassured that ancient Israel really did not mean this or take it seriously. We do not know; there are many reviews of the suggested evidence for such a practice that are not decisive concerning the historicity of the regulation. Be that as it may, it is in the tradition, and that it was imagined and remembered is enough to see that debt was kept penultimate in a covenantal milieu, that is, in the memory of exodus-Sinai.

Because the provision of Deuteronomy 15:1 is stated so starkly and radically, we can see why it received, in the text, extended elucidation. Verses 2–3 delineate between "neighbor" and "foreigner." As we shall see in several places, the foreigner can be treated according to conventional economics, but not the neighbor, that is, a fellow member of the covenant community. It is for that reason that the wonderment, "Who is my neighbor?," looms so large in the tradition.

It is clear in what follows in the text that the initial provision concerned all debtors, but the focus of interest is on the needy, the ones likely to be burdened with insurmountable debt. Thus the needy are front and center in verses 4, 7, 8, and 11. Economic matters must yield to social reality; and the social reality is that if the needy are kept in debt, they cannot be viable neighbors. The regulation is clearly addressed to creditors. Israel's creditors belong in a vast company of creditors. As David Graeber recounts in his history of debt:

For thousands of years, the struggle between rich and poor has largely taken the form of conflicts between creditors and debtors—of arguments about the rights and wrongs of interest payments, debt peonage, amnesty, repossession, restitution, the sequestering of sheep, the seizing of vineyards, and the selling of debtors' children into slavery. By the same token, for the last five thousand years, with remarkable regularity, popular insurrections have begun the same way: with the ritual destruction of the debt records—tablets, papyri, ledgers, whatever form they might have taken in any particular place . . . all revolutionary movements had a single program: "Cancel the debts, burn the records, and redistribute the land."[4]

This address to creditors as a summons, moreover, is not welcome. Moses urges that creditors should not be "hard-hearted or tight-fisted" (v. 7), a condition that is likely if money is understood apart from the infrastructure of neighborliness. The warning against being "hard-hearted" could be an allusion to Pharaoh in his acquisitiveness, for he is the quintessential agent with a hard heart.

The urgency of the regulation is indicated in the exposition by the utilization of seven absolute infinitive verbs. This is an intensification of the verb in Hebrew whereby the verb is repeated a second time. Unfortunately it is impossible to render this in a recognizable form in English. Thus the infinitive absolutes:

> Sure to bless (v. 4)
> Really obey (v. 5)
> Really give (v. 8)
> Willingly lend (v. 8)
> Give liberally (v. 10)
> Really open (v. 11)
> Provide liberally (v. 14)

This mass of seven intensive verbs, unparalleled elsewhere in Scripture as far as I know, is a measure of how important this provision is in the tradition:

There will, however, be no one in need among you, because the LORD is sure to bless you in the land that the LORD your God is giving you as a possession to occupy, if only you will obey the

LORD your God by diligently observing this entire commandment that I command you today. When the LORD your God has blessed you, as he promised you, you will lend to many nations, but you will not borrow; you will rule over many nations, but they will not rule over you.

If there is among you anyone in need, a member of your community in any of your towns within the land that the LORD your God is giving you, do not be hard-hearted or tight-fisted toward your needy neighbor. You should rather open your hand, willingly lending enough to meet the need, whatever it may be. Be careful that you do not entertain a mean thought, thinking, "The seventh year, the year of remission, is near," and therefore view your needy neighbor with hostility and give nothing; your neighbor might cry to the LORD against you, and you would incur guilt. Give liberally and be ungrudging when you do so, for on this account the LORD your God will bless you in all your work and in all that you undertake. Since there will never cease to be some in need on the earth, I therefore command you, "Open your hand to the poor and needy neighbor in your land."

If a member of your community, whether a Hebrew man or a Hebrew woman, is sold to you and works for you six years, in the seventh year you shall set that person free. And when you send a male slave out from you a free person, you shall not send him out empty-handed. Provide liberally out of your flock, your threshing floor, and your wine press, thus giving to him some of the bounty with which the LORD your God has blessed you. Remember that you were a slave in the land of Egypt, and the LORD your God redeemed you; for this reason I lay this command upon you today. (vv. 4–15)

We are, in this regulation, at the heart of biblical teaching about wealth and possessions, a regulation that wealth is held provisionally, and debt cannot become a permanent lever of the economy. The most radical teaching of the Bible on wealth and possessions concerns forgiveness of debts, for debt over time erodes neighborliness and makes viable social life impossible.

Two statements in the exposition of the commandment, when juxtaposed, become especially interesting. In verse 4 it is asserted that "there will be no one in need among you," that is, no one without resources who remains in debt. That is, the practice of this regulation will eliminate economic debts. The reason that there will be no needy is that the resources of the community are distributed, not according to personal property, but according to social solidarity. The rhetoric of verse 4 is juxtaposed to the more familiar statement of verse 11: "There will never cease to be some in need on the earth." Or more familiarly, "The poor you will always have with you."

This is not a statement of resignation, as it is often taken to be. It is rather an underscoring about why this provision must be practiced with faithfulness. Thus verse 4 promises that poverty can be overcome; verse 11 asserts that continual attentiveness to the poor and needy is urgent. They can never be left in a vulnerable state, but are entitled to protection and a viable life in the community. The grounding for this urgent regulation, of course, is a remembrance of the exodus (v. 15).

IV

To make the connection for our time and circumstance, all that is required is to see that death and adversity come from not obeying the commands of neighborliness, that is, by succumbing to the social vision of the Canaanites and, before the Canaanites, the social vision of Pharaoh. Alternative life and prosperity come from obedience to Torah commands, that is, to neighborly practice, especially toward widows, orphans, and immigrants.

Questions for Reflection

1. The Deuteronomic tradition entails a never-ending practice of authorizing, empowering, and envisioning neighborliness. This new way of being is difficult to integrate into our everyday lives. What would it mean to be a part of this work and what would it expect of you? Ponder this for a moment and write down your thoughts.

2. The commandments subvert self-serving economies and reorient us to practices and relationships that enhance community and support those who are most vulnerable. Offerings and tithing are also a part of this subversion. How does this make you rethink the concepts

of "offerings" and "tithes"? How might this change the way your church uses its financial gifts?

3. At the heart of biblical teachings concerning wealth and possessions is the principle that debt cannot be a permanent player in any economy, because it most impacts those who are most vulnerable. Societal relationships deteriorate. Cultivating a neighborhood is almost impossible. What are your own views on debt? Where do you see debt eroding relationships in your own life? In the lives of others?

4. "The poor you will always have with you," Jesus said, a statement that Brueggemann notes is often read as one of resignation. How have you been taught to read this passage? How does this understanding shift in light of the author's emphasis on Deuteronomy's command to act faithfully toward the needy through the forgiveness of debts?

PART FOUR

The Ongoing Imagination
of Liberation

Chapter 9

Resistors to and Advocates for Biblical Salvation

*T*hreats to biblical salvation do not come only from apparently external opponents such as Pharaonic Egypt and Canaanite city-states. There is also a powerful *counternarrative* in the biblical tradition that resists the claims of exodus-Sinai-Deuteronomy. It is a counternarrative that resists the neighbor question, because the drawback into the fearful, anxious world of Pharaoh is enormously compelling for almost all of us. Our memory fades, and we imagine the security that Pharaoh's system offered and yearn for an imagined well-being back there.

I

Once they had arrived at Sinai, we can see a much more sustained effort to resist the emancipatory narrative of neighborliness. The travel out of Egypt into the alternative narrative immediately produces an attack of nostalgia for the imagined good old days of Pharaoh. Israel had found the new narrative too demanding and too precarious, and failed in their feeble remembering. As the tradition is shaped from Mount Sinai, this resistance to the emancipatory narrative is advanced by the purity trajectory. The purity traditions may have come late, but now they are lodged right in the midst of the Sinai corpus itself (Exod. 25–31; 35–40; Leviticus; Num. 10:11–36:13). In the development of *holiness* as a qualification for access to God's gifts for life, there came the notion of "graded holiness," that is, that there are degrees of eligibility, so that some are more eligible for access than others.[1] Israel appropriates from its cultural environment a pattern of organizing holy space with three "chambers of qualification," so that there will be an outer court, a holy place, and a most holy place (holy of holies), where there is an intensity of divine presence and divine power. The chambers are ordered so that some are admitted only at the edge, fewer are permitted to enter midway, and only one is given access clear to the center. The process differentiates between neighbors, some better than others.

As close as we can come to such a notion of three chambers of qualification is a commercial airline with tourist class and first class, and the "holy of holies" where none may go (more recently protected by a very strong door).[2] But, of course, every social organization has differentiations among neighbors, sometimes regional, sometimes educational, sometimes race, class, and gender, and sometimes ideological. At Sinai some imagined the regimentation of holiness concerned:

- *Cultic access*—which is like health care policy—since the priests were the doctors of that time, administrators of health care.
- *Moral ratings*, good people and bad people, clean people and unclean people, a Manichean perspective that continues to vex communities, liberal and conservative, the rational and the passionate.
- *Economic possibility* for those who have access to resources and opportunity in the neighborhood. The gradations of holiness concerning economic possibility tend to turn on connectedness, being at the right place at the right time, and productivity. Consequently those who are not productive are increasingly banished from access to the goodies.

The resistance to the common good has *cultic*, *moral*, and *economic* dimensions. As a consequence, we can, in broad outline, see a collision course between the *neighborly possibilities* mandated by the tradition of Deuteronomy and the *regimentations of holiness* in the Priestly traditions. Both are in the Bible; both are at Sinai. We may imagine, moreover, that this ancient folk, like us, are of a double mind about it. They knew better, but when it came down to cases, they could not help making distinctions. Thus we may imagine that even given the exodus Sinai narrative of an alternative to Pharaoh's system, there was a struggle concerning the neighborly good. That struggle eventuated in an interpretive contest, a contest kept alive among Jews in the rabbinic traditions of Hillel and Gamaliel, and on into our own time among contemporary orthodox and rationalistic interpretations. Contestation for the common good is an endless project. That contest is a summons and a vexation in the church, because of our own double-mindedness.

II

The exodus-Sinai narrative for neighborliness holds center stage in the Old Testament. It is with King Solomon, however, that this narrative faces its most serious challenge. In Solomon there is (a) a fresh *enthrallment with Egypt* and (b) a passion for *graded holiness*. There is, moreover, a deep connection between these two, for Pharaoh's Egyptian society did indeed practice graded holiness with its cultic, moral, and economic dimensions (see Gen. 43:32 on discriminating lunch-counter practices). Had Israel remembered better, they would have remembered more clearly what it was like back in Egypt to be graded at the lowest level and therefore denied access to economic benefit. There is something ironic about this most prominent king in ancient Israel; his name "Solomon" means shalom, but his sponsorship of a skewed royal shalom contradicts the common good.[3]

The echoes of Pharaoh's exploitative system are everywhere evident in what we know about Solomon. For starters, the king is married to Pharaoh's daughter and surely wants to borrow from and emulate his father-in-law (see 1 Kgs. 3:1; 7:8; 9:16, 24). It is most plausible that there were important imports from Egypt by Solomon, not least his policy of forced labor that conscripted people to support the aggrandizing projects of the government. That conscription we now call "the draft," but in ancient days and in ancient texts it is termed "forced labor" (1 Sam. 8:10–17; 1 Kgs. 5:13–18; 9:20–22). It is evident that Pharaoh's notion of the common good—a hierarchical ordering shaped like an Egyptian pyramid—reappeared in Jerusalem.

The echoes of Pharaoh are matched by a graded holiness and by its consequent of a hierarchical ordering of society. Solomon, of course, is the great temple builder in ancient Israel. We have, in the text, what amounts to a blueprint for his temple that was an imitation of a generic type of building from his culture:

- The "outer court," in NRSV, is called "the vestibule":

  The vestibule in front of the nave of the house was twenty cubits wide, across the width of the house. Its depth was ten cubits in front of the house. (1 Kgs. 6:3)

- The "holy court," in NRSV, is called "the nave":

  He also built a structure against the wall of the house, running around the walls of the house, both the nave and the inner sanctuary; and he made side chambers all around. The lowest story was five cubits wide, the middle one was six cubits wide, and the third was seven cubits wide; for around the outside of the house he made offsets on the wall in order that the supporting beams should not be inserted into the walls of the house. . . . The house, that is, the nave in front of the inner sanctuary, was forty cubits long. The cedar within the house had carvings of gourds and open flowers; all was cedar, no stone was seen. (vv. 5–6, 17–18)

- The "holy of holies," in NRSV, is called "the most holy place":

  He built twenty cubits of the rear of the house with boards of cedar from the floor to the rafters, and he built this within as an inner sanctuary, as the most holy place. . . . The inner sanctuary he prepared in the innermost part of the house, to set there the ark of the covenant of the Lord. The interior of the inner sanctuary was twenty cubits long, twenty cubits wide, and twenty cubits high; he overlaid it with pure *gold*. He also overlaid the altar with cedar. Solomon overlaid the inside of the house with pure *gold*, then he drew chains of *gold* across, in front of the inner sanctuary, and overlaid it with *gold*. Next he overlaid the whole house with *gold*, in order that the whole house might be perfect; even the whole altar that belonged to the inner sanctuary he overlaid with *gold*. (vv. 16, 19–22, emphasis added)

I take so long with this matter because the shape of the temple wrought by Solomon is not an accidental architectural detail. It is, rather, a replica of *an imagined social order*. That the description of the temple ends with the term *gold* used six times indicates a fascination with precious commodity; by extrapolation we may conclude that Solomon's temple was committed to the commoditization of all social relationships so that we are able to see *what* is valued and, consequently, *who* is valued. (It is the shape and arrangement of airplanes, school systems, health-care delivery, housing patterns, and all the rest.)

Solomon's fascination with all things Egyptian and Solomon's zeal for the temple with its older residence for God invite us to look closely at the royal report from which we can determine a great deal about the socioeconomic claims of this narrative, which stands in deep tension with the neighborly narrative of Sinai.

I will identify three aspects of this narrative of royal regime that are important for the long-term claims of faith:

- It is clear that Solomon is committed to an accumulation of *wealth*, that everything in his hand turned commodity. The temple reeks with gold, and after his summit meeting with the Queen of Sheba, we are told:

  Thus King Solomon excelled all the kings of the earth in riches and in wisdom. . . . Every one of them brought a present, objects of silver and gold, garments, weaponry, spices, horses, and mules, so much year by year. (10:23, 25; see vv. 14–20)

It may well be that the acquisitiveness and commoditization are also reflected in the report that Solomon had seven hundred princesses and three hundred concubines (11:3). The numbers might suggest that this throng of women were used, if not for sexual purposes, then surely for political purposes through a network of alliances.

- It is clear that Solomon is committed to *power*. It is evident that his power was linked to his wealth. His enormous power is expressed in the fact that he was an arms dealer, a middleman passing horses and chariots between north and south:

> Solomon's import of horses was from Egypt and Kue, and the king's traders received them from Kue at a price. A chariot could be imported from Egypt for six hundred shekels of silver, and a horse for one hundred fifty; so through the king's traders they were exported to all the kings of the Hittites and the kings of Aram. (10:28–29)

It is astonishing that much arms traffic, then and now, is not in the service of any policy; it is, rather, simply a way of financial leverage. Alongside Solomon's traffic in armaments, he had immense commercial interest (9:26–28), plus a system of collecting protection money from a variety of sources:

> Solomon was sovereign over all the kingdoms from the Euphrates to the land of the Philistines, even to the border of Egypt; they brought tribute and served Solomon all the days of his life. (4:21)

His commercial power was matched and reinforced by his military power, as he kept a standing army of chariots and cavalry, and built immense fortresses at the key locations of Hazor, Gezer, and Megiddo:

> This is the account of the forced labor that King Solomon conscripted to build the house of the LORD and his own house, the Millo and the wall of Jerusalem, Hazor, Megiddo, Gezer, . . . Lower Beth-horon, Baalath, Tamar in the wilderness, within the land, as well as all of Solomon's storage cities, the cities for his chariots, the cities for his cavalry, and whatever Solomon desired to build, in Jerusalem, in Lebanon, and in all the land of his dominion. (9:15, 17–19)

The practice of forced labor, commoditization, traffic in arms, and commerce through trade agreements all converged to make Solomon a major political force in his world, a fact attested by his meeting with the Queen of Sheba, which was surely a summit concerning trade agreements (10:1–10). Solomon did indeed fashion a national security state!

- Solomon is a great practitioner of *wisdom*. It is reported that he composed three hundred proverbs and one hundred and five songs:

He would speak of trees, from the cedar that is in the Lebanon to the hyssop that grows in the wall; he would speak of animals, and birds, and reptiles, and fish. People came from all the nations to hear the wisdom of Solomon; they came from all the kings of the earth who had heard of his wisdom. (4:33–34)

We may take this as his personal achievement. More likely it is a celebration of Solomon as a patron of the arts, not unlike having Isaac Stern at the White House. Solomon's artists included the poets of wisdom who were able to codify what became scientific data concerning "creation." The quest for "wisdom" may have been (a) in order to appear as champion of the arts that would enhance the regime, (b) the development of the arts and skills of governance that depended on a practice of discernment, and (c) the accumulation of data so that the elite had a monopoly on "intelligence." All of these interests in art, governance, and intelligence converge in "wisdom," for which Solomon is noted. While such wisdom may have a theological component, given Solomon's pursuit of wealth and power, we may take "wisdom" here in a more cynical sense as a practice of control. Solomon is celebrated for his worldly awareness, perhaps in the same way as the "wise men" that clustered around Lyndon Johnson and Richard Nixon, of whom Henry Kissinger is, as of this writing, the last prominent survivor.[4] These are the ones, then and now, who knew everything but in the end failed to understand anything:

The whole earth sought the presence of Solomon to hear his wisdom, which God had put into his mind. (10:24)

Solomon understood how the world worked, probed the mysteries, and kept on his payroll the academics who could advance his control, his prestige, and his security.

There is a reason that Solomon is so celebrated and so widely admired. He is, as remembered in the narrative, the prominent man, "the man," who embodies *the best* control of the world, for what is better than a collage of *wealth, power,* and *wisdom*! The consequence is that one can have the world on one's own terms.

Now having summarized all of that as a counternarrative that by design and in effect resisted the exodus-Sinai narrative, I conclude

my comment on Solomon with an interesting footnote. At the beginning of the Solomon narrative there is an ironic report on the hand-
over of power from the father David to his son Solomon. In 2:2–4
David soberly admonishes Solomon to keep the Torah as the basis
of the throne. This advice from David is followed immediately with
David's urging to Solomon that he immediately and systematically
execute his enemies in the government, Joab and Shimei (vv. 5–8). It
is reported, moreover, that Solomon palpably did so, eliminating not
only Joab and Shimei, as David had urged (vv. 28–46), but also his
brother Adonijah (vv. 13–25), a rival for the family throne.

What interests us is that in the midst of these assassinations
enacted in order to secure the throne, there is a brief paragraph about
Abiathar, the priest who had opposed Solomon's kingship (see 1:7).
He is a dangerous opponent of Solomon, but you cannot kill a priest
. . . yet! Instead of a death sentence, Abiathar is banished by Solomon
away from the capital city to his home village, where he cannot do
any harm to the regime:

> The king said to the priest Abiathar, "Go to Anathoth, to your
> estate; for you deserve death. But I will not at this time put you
> to death, because you carried the ark of the Lord GOD before my
> father David, and because you shared in all the hardships my
> father endured." So Solomon banished Abiathar from being priest
> to the LORD, thus fulfilling the word of the LORD that he had spo-
> ken concerning the house of Eli in Shiloh. (2:26–27)

Abiathar departs the regime of *wealth, power, and wisdom* and is
marginalized in his innocent, remote village, there to watch the
regime and to brood about its commitments to distortion. He will
have a very long time to brood . . . but I will leave that for now.

III

Solomon is the model in the Bible for a global perspective of the common good, a perspective that smacks of *privilege, entitlement,* and
exploitation, all in the name of the God of the three-chambered temple,
the three chambers that partition social life and social resources into
the qualified, the partially qualified, and *the disqualified.* It takes little

critical imagination to see that Solomon's perspective, which came to dominate urban Israel's imagination, is an act of resistance against the neighborly demands of Sinai, and an alternative to the possibilities of Mount Sinai. It is as though Pharaoh, through his son-in-law, had come to rule in Israel as in Egypt. Jerusalem becomes a place that reenacts Pharaoh's acquisitiveness that is rooted in Pharaoh's anxieties. That perspective of Pharaoh-via-Solomon takes on a powerful life in Jerusalem, largely nullifying the vision of Sinai. In the end it is as though the exodus had never happened. Or as Moses says, at the end of the book of Deuteronomy in the ultimate covenant curse, it is as though the alternative possibility for God's people is to end, yet again, in Egypt:

> The LORD will bring you back in ships to Egypt, by a route that I promised you would never see again; and there you shall offer yourselves for sale to your enemies as male and female slaves, but there will be no buyer. (Deut. 28:68)

Pharaoh always prevails! Except that Sinai continues to have its advocates. The advocates in ancient Israel are not shrill administrators. They are, rather, poets who imagine outside the box, who, by their very lives, attest that the world can be organized differently. You know the roll call of those poets who did not give in to Pharaoh. The list is short!

- *Nathan*, who by way of parable faced Solomonic, pharaonic King David (2 Sam. 12:1–5)
- *Elijah*, reckoned as "troubler" and "enemy" in Israel (1 Kgs. 18:17; 21:20), who dealt with Solomonic, pharaonic Ahab
- *Amos*, who grieved a failed society in his confrontation with Solomonic, pharaonic Amaziah (Amos 7:10–17)

The prophets were not great liberals. They were, rather, *poets* outside the box who were rooted in Sinai, who were gifted with uncommon imagination, and who operated on the astonishing notion that the claims of the exodus God who had created heaven and earth were not easily overcome or dismissed. They were, each in a distinct style and context, convinced that the common good was ill served by Solomon's chambers of qualification or by pharaonic notions of cheap labor in the interest of a predatory economy.

IV

If one studies the Old Testament, one can see a collision course in ancient Israel, long in coming but certainly not to be escaped. The Jerusalem enterprise was increasingly narcoticized by its sense of entitlement; it imagined itself exempt from the starchy requirements of the historical process, and so delivered to its beneficiaries a wondrous entitlement of privilege and security under the aegis of a patron God.

But the poets notice! And if you draw the Old Testament down toward its 9/11 crisis of the destruction of Jerusalem in 587 BCE, you eventually will come to the prophet Jeremiah, who, in his poetic daring, had to preside over his 9/11—for it takes a poet to comprehend such profound loss! Imagine, it is not the managers, not the ideologues, not the social activists, not the shrill moralists, right or left, but the poets, who are able (and compelled!) to go to the depth of the crisis and to reach deep into God's own conflicted heart.[5]

Jeremiah is a village guy with not very impressive credentials. The book of Jeremiah begins with his pedigree:

> The words of Jeremiah son of Hilkiah, of the priests who were in Anathoth in the land of Benjamin. (Jer. 1:1)

He is the son of Hilkiah, a priest. He was from the land of Benjamin, just across the northern border from Judah and Jerusalem, close enough to see, far enough to be unencumbered. Hilkiah, his father, we may know only from one other text. Perhaps he was the priest who helped recover the scroll of Deuteronomy for King Josiah (2 Kgs. 22:8–13). Benjamin we know in ancient geography. But in that opening line, between Hilkiah and Benjamin stands . . . Anathoth! The utterance of the word "Anathoth" sets off among us an exegetical alarm. We know of this village hometown; we reel through our exegetical memory bank and push back to the verses concerning Solomon's seizure of power. The verdict of the aggressive new king to the honored old priest Abiathar:

> Go to Anathoth, to your estate; for you deserve death. (1 Kgs. 2:26)

Abiathar went to Anathoth, defrocked from Jerusalem, still a rural priest acting as a village pastor. He had sons, and sons of sons. They were, like him, priests. They did that for four hundred years. Every day, for four hundred years, they looked to the southern horizon of the village. They could see traces of Jerusalem, and they heard the reports. They heard reports of forced labor and armaments and political marriages and exploitation and foolishness of a hundred kinds. Coming from the city were the mantras that mingled exclusive religion and patriotic exceptionalism, affirmations about *unconditional promise* (2 Sam. 7:15–16), and an *uninterrupted divine presence* (1 Kgs. 8:12–13) (and "bombs bursting in air and rockets' red glare"), and abusive labor policy and despair and anxiety and self-sufficiency and amnesia and, finally, an illusion. It took four hundred years to gather together a sinking sense of an ending.

At the end of four hundred years, this son of exiled Abiathar—many generations later—this son of exiles from Jerusalem, this Jeremiah, showed up in Jerusalem yet again. The man from Anathoth showed up there with his own words: "Jeremiah, . . . to whom the word of the LORD came" (Jer. 1:1–2). He has spent four hundred years transposing the word of the Lord into the words of Jeremiah. It was a word evoked exactly for this moment. He addresses the kings who managed the establishment:

> . . . in the days of King Josiah son of Amon of Judah, in the thirteenth year of his reign. It came also in the days of King Jehoiakim son of Josiah of Judah . . . (vv. 2–3)

It was a word to the establishment that could see beyond the kings, so that his opener ended this way:

> . . . until the end of the eleventh year of King Zedekiah son of Josiah of Judah, until the captivity of Jerusalem in the fifth month. (v. 3)

This is a word from the banished poet to the kings, until their royal displacement. The poet brings only words. But what else will matter when the city crackles in flames and the leadership is seized by an ending that they did not see coming? Jeremiah and his family had watched—for four hundred years—and had long since seen a trajectory of death. That trajectory was marked by

- Solomonic wealth: "gold, gold, gold"
- Solomonic power, so that there was no one like him, before or since (1 Kgs. 3:12)
- Solomonic wisdom, ample proverbs, and files of intelligence

It was a trajectory to death. It was a long-term practice of the lethal. Opposition and resistance to the lethal does not require more technology or more advocacy or more activism. It simply evokes words of a special sort:

> The words of Jeremiah . . . to whom the word of the LORD came.

V

Jeremiah, with a deep breath, decisively counters the primal commitments of the Jerusalem establishment. We can see in one poetic-prophetic utterance the collision of these two perceptions of reality. Here is the poem:

> Thus says the LORD: Do not let the wise boast in their *wisdom*, do not let the mighty boast in their *might*, do not let the wealthy boast in their *wealth*; but let those who boast boast in this, that they understand and know me, that I am the LORD; I act with *steadfast love*, *justice*, and *righteousness* in the earth, for in these things I delight, says the LORD. (Jer. 9:23–24, emphasis added)

The poem is in five parts. I spend time on it, because I have come to think that these are the verses that provide the clue to the ancient 9/11 in Jeremiah's time and perhaps to our own time and place as God's people:

1. Jeremiah lines out *the lethal commitments* that are at work in the Jerusalem establishment:

- Do not praise wealth.
- Do not praise might.
- Do not praise wisdom.

The term *boast*—"do not let the wise boast"—is the Hebrew term *hallel*, as in *hallelu-jah*, "praise YHWH." Do not commend or celebrate these qualities of life.

It is as though, in this triad of wealth, might, and wisdom, the poet has simply taken a page from Solomon's playbook. You will remember Solomon's inventory of achievements:

- enough *wisdom* to control the mystery and to reduce it to a technical operation
- enough *might* to build a national security state in the middle of the Fertile Crescent
- enough *wealth* to satisfy every acquisitive appetite

Enough of wisdom, might, and wealth; and says Jeremiah, "Don't brag on it!"

2. There is, says the village poet, *an alternative*:

[B]ut let those who boast boast in this, that they understand and know me, that I am the LORD. (Jer. 9:24)

Now the term *hallel* might be "praise" rather than "boast." The big issue in the "boast" that is now recommended is that it refers to YHWH, the God of the exodus. The double list of "boasts" is an *either-or* in ancient Jerusalem, mutually exclusive, YHWH or the Solomonic triad. But this alternative is more than a claim for YHWH; it is also a claim for Israel. Israel is the community that "knows YHWH," that is privy to YHWH's purpose in the world and has committed to YHWH. As a result Israel "understands" YHWH, reflects deeply upon who YHWH is. The "or" of the "either-or" is to meditate on the Torah, which constitutes the ground of knowledge and discernment concerning YHWH. Imagine that—something Pharaoh never thought about and over which Solomon never lingered: access to YHWH's own life in the world.

3. The end of the sentence is "*I am YHWH*." In the world of wealth, might, and wisdom, everyone is an object or a commodity that occurs at the end of the sentence. But when YHWH occurs at the end of a sentence in that frame of reference, YHWH is transposed into a lifeless idol. That is what Solomon sought and finally accomplished in his third chamber—a God settled, under control, tamed to a favorite ideology, echo of a preferred social passion. But not here in Jeremiah. Here *YHWH is the subject and not the object*, an agent and not a commodity, a force of will and not an idol. Thus

the text has YHWH say, "I am YHWH who . . ." I am YHWH who creates heaven and earth. I am YHWH who brought you out of the land of Egypt. I am YHWH who heals all your diseases and forgives all your sins. I am YHWH who creates and re-creates. Such a God cannot function easily in a world of three-chambered qualification, of systemic and absolute control. Such a God lives in tension with the royal triad and with pet projects of any sort.

4. YHWH is the one *with active verbs*. YHWH is the one with remarkable adjectives:

> I act with steadfast love, justice, and righteousness in the earth, for in these things I delight, says the LORD. (v. 24)

So here is YHWH's triad, which we first might state in Hebrew: *hesed, mishpat, tsedaqah.*

- *Steadfast love* (*hesed*) is to stand in solidarity, to honor commitments, to be reliable toward all the partners.
- *Justice* (*mishpat*) in the Old Testament concerns distribution in order to make sure that all members of the community have access to resources and goods for the sake of a viable life of dignity. In covenantal tradition the particular subject of YHWH's justice is the triad "widow, orphan, immigrant," those without leverage or muscle to sustain their own legitimate place in society.
- *Righteousness* (*tsedaqah*) concerns active intervention in social affairs, taking an initiative to intervene effectively in order to rehabilitate society, to respond to social grievance, and to correct every humanity-diminishing activity.

This triad—*hesed, mishpat,* and *tsedaqah*—is everywhere present in Old Testament talk about divine purpose and about Israel's covenantal life in the world. The terms, moreover, overlap and cover for one another, so that when any one of them occurs in the text, we may extrapolate to the others. The God of Israel, unlike the gods of Egypt, is committed to the covenantal project of each in solidarity for all. And Israel, pledged to YHWH, is committed to the same project.

5. Finally, Jeremiah has God say at the end of the passage, "In these things—in *hesed,* in *mishpat,* in *tsedaqah*—I delight."

The term *delight* is a word used in prophetic poetry to describe the kinds of offerings and sacrifices that are offered in worship that will please YHWH. Indeed, it is the same term used in Hosea 6:6, where the prophet prioritizes covenantal solidarity over cultic activity:

> For I *desire* steadfast love and not sacrifice,
> the knowledge of God rather than burnt offerings.

This text, moreover, is reiterated twice by Jesus:

- In Matthew 9:13, in the debate over eating with tax collectors and sinners:

  > Go and learn what this means, "I *desire* mercy, not sacrifice." For I have come to call not the righteous but sinners.

- In 12:7, with the debate over healing on the Sabbath:

  > But if you had known what this means, "I *desire* mercy and not sacrifice," you would not have condemned the guiltless.

In Jeremiah 9, in Hosea 6, and twice in the teaching of Jesus according to Matthew, it is the faithful well-being of the human community that is *well pleasing to YHWH*:

> YHWH loves steadfast covenantal solidarity.
> YHWH loves justice that gives access and viability to the weak.
> YHWH loves righteousness as intervention for social well-being.

And, says the prophet, you in covenant are the ones who can brag on this, that you have been given the secret of God's primal impulse.

VI

Finally, as I have pondered Sinai and Solomon and the two great triads, I have thought about Jesus' words to his disciples about anxiety and not having it both ways:

> No one can serve two masters; for a slave will either hate the one and love the other, or be devoted to the one and despise the other. You cannot serve God and wealth.
>
> Therefore I tell you, do not worry about your life, what you will eat or what you will drink, or about your body, what you will wear. Is not life more than food, and the body more than clothing? (Matt. 6:24–25)

Jesus understands that his disciples were a lot like the world in their several anxieties. He urges them to be different, to be more like trustful creatures (lilies and birds) and less like acquisitive operators. He observes the easy trust and the daily responsiveness of lilies and birds and then he says, in one of his most remarkable utterances:

> Yet I tell you, even Solomon in all his glory was not clothed like one of these. (v. 29)

Solomon! Solomon of the great triad of wisdom, might, and wealth! Be unlike Solomon in pursuit of control and domination and safety. Be unlike the triad of Pharaoh, unlike the triad of the national security state, unlike the triad of old certitudes:

> For it is the Gentiles who strive for all these things; and indeed your heavenly Father knows that you need all these things. But strive first for the kingdom of God and his righteousness, and all these things will be given to you as well. (vv. 32–33)

The cadences of *hesed*, *mishpat*, and *tsedaqah* continue to sound. They are a minority voice of subversion and alternative, and they have been entrusted to us.

Questions for Reflection

1. Our own double-mindedness creates hierarchies of holiness within our churches and in our own lives. In what ways have you seen this differentiation happen in your life and in the life of your church?

2. Solomon was a man of wisdom, power, and wealth. Our traditions have praised him for these attributes, and as a man who knew the world and placed a high value on intellect. Do you see these values

reflected in your life? In your tradition? Why have we elevated these things as necessary to understand the world and the life of faith?

3. The prophets (Amos, Elijah, Nathan, etc.) were poets who were rooted in neighborly imagination and spoke out against qualification, differentiation, and economic exploitation. In what ways are you, or can you be, a poetic force against a predatory economy? Imagine for a moment creative ways to be prophetic in your own context and church.

4. The triad of *hesed*, *mishpat*, and *tsedaqah*—steadfast love, justice, and righteousness—are not to be isolated from each other; they are intimately connected, integral to the character of God, and point us toward neighborliness. How is this triad manifesting in your life?

Chapter 10

The Economic Core
of Prophetic Criticism

The previous chapter explores how the prophets could constitute great disruptive forces against both internal and external threats to ancient Israel's salvation. They consistently rearticulate the promise of salvation made possible through the God of the exodus, the realization of which they poetically reimagine through various modes of social organization similar to those mandated by God at Sinai and repurposed by Moses in Deuteronomy. Not all prophets fulfilled this characteristic function, and at times others who were not prophets contributed to these efforts. Nevertheless, by daring, often outrageous, poetic image and metaphor, prophetic utterance repeatedly disrupts what seems to be a settled society with alternative visions of God's salvation.

I

The prophets regularly appear in social circumstances where an organizing power exercises hegemonic control. Among the prophets of the eighth and seventh centuries BCE, that hegemonic control was exercised by the royal regimes in Samaria, capital city of northern Israel (see Amos 7:10–17), and much more powerfully by the Jerusalem establishment that featured royal power enhanced by priestly and scribal functionaries. These hegemonic regimes fostered a kind of absolutism that was grounded in a claim of chosenness, so that visible power was supported by ideological posturing. The royal apparatus, north and south, sought to make a claim for legitimacy that refused any disruption and fostered a kind of self-sufficiency.

In the sixth century, by contrast, hegemonic control featured Babylonian governance, to be later displaced by Persian rule. These empires practiced domination and seemed guaranteed in perpetuity. Among the displaced Jewish population, such imperial control generated disappointment and despair, as the regimes appeared to be beyond disruption.

Both the royal regimes of Samaria and Jerusalem and the imperial regimes of Babylon and Persia were, in varying degrees, committed to economic extraction from the common population to produce surplus wealth for the governing elite, who had arranged the economy for their own benefit. Thus in eighth- and seventh-century Israel-Judah and in sixth-century Babylon and Persia, a kind of totalism was established that kept *a process of economic extraction* closely linked to *an ideological hegemony* that produced a closed sociopolitical system.

The emergence of the prophets in that context is a remarkable social phenomenon in which voices from elsewhere, from outside the totalism, sounded with immense authority that defied and displaced the authority of the regimes with the claim of authority of the creator God who rendered all other authority penultimate.[1] Thus prophetic utterance, with a claim to transcendent authority, voiced an alternative view of social life; the world they voiced featured YHWH, the Lord of the covenant and the guarantor of justice, as the true governor of all social reality, including especially the economy. The prophetic corpus offers a sustained critique of an economy of extraction that thrived in the kingdoms of Samaria and Jerusalem and in the larger imperial powers that displaced those kingdoms. On the one hand, such subversive speech countered the self-congratulatory governance of Samaria and Jerusalem. On the other hand, such intrusive speech countered the governance of empire that had resulted in despair for the Jewish population.

When viewed as an interruption of totalism, it is not surprising that prophetic speech is characteristically poetic speech that abounds in playful imagery and metaphor. Settled political-economic power tends to converse in memos that are designed for control without slippage. In order to interrupt the tight world of memos, prophetic speech employs poetry that refuses the logic of hegemony and that generates imagined social possibilities that turn out to be deeply subversive.[2] Such elusive utterance refuses and resists every absolutism. This daring speech, however, does not suggest that it is lacking in social realism, for these prophetic voices evidence an acute practice of social analysis. It is not too much to say, I believe, that these poets rather consistently followed the money in a culture of extraction, for they knew that the ultimate intent of the creator God—expressed in the traditions of covenant—was for a neighborly economy. They knew, further, that performance of a just economy as a real social possibility represented an acute challenge to settled social power, an almost unthinkable alternative that required emancipated speech for its actualization. Thus prophetic utterance is speech that disrupts totalism, is grounded in divine alternative, and is voiced as emancipatory alternative.

The prophetic books consist, through a process of editing, of a collection of such utterances that are remembered and treasured and found always again to offer a fresh contemporaneity. We may imagine that such utterances were variously random and ad hoc as socioeconomic crises evoked them. But of course such random and ad hoc utterances, through the canonical process, have been intentionally ordered to give shape and body to the paradigmatic history of Israel. That paradigmatic history, which stands a bit distant from reportable history, consists in (a) the *destruction of Jerusalem* as the epitome of failed chosenness and the descent into the abyss of displacement, deportation, and loss, and (b) the promised *restoration of Jerusalem* and the anticipated homecoming of the displaced to their true homeland. This model of *displacement and restoration* has provided the pattern of the canonical ordering of the prophetic books:

> We can at least come to understand the value and meaning of the way in which distinctive patterns have been imposed upon the prophetic collections of the canon so that warnings of doom and disaster are always followed by promises of hope and restoration. . . . This centered on the death and rebirth of Israel, interpreted theologically as acts of divine judgment and salvation.[3]

Thus ordered and rendered, the ad hoc utterances now voice a paradigmatic constant that in Judaism concerns *exile and homecoming* and in Christian tradition has been transposed into *crucifixion and resurrection*, which concerns not only Jesus but also the life of the world.

This canonical pattern is evident in the several prophetic books as they characteristically begin in *harsh judgment* and end in *buoyant anticipation of recovery*. When this patterned canonical sequence is seen in terms of our theme of biblical salvation, it comes to be expressed as (a) the harsh termination of the practice of social exploitation and economic extraction and (b) the prospect of a new socioeconomic life that will be funded by divine generosity and practiced as neighborly justice. The entire process from *ad hoc particular utterance* to *canonical pattern* serves to connect divine purpose and actual concrete practice. That connection is uncompromisingly *subversive* of status quo hegemony and compellingly *anticipatory* of an alternative socioeconomic possibility outside the structures and strategies of hegemonic regimes.

II

A predominant theme of the prophetic corpus is the conviction that a predatory economy that permits powerful moneyed interests to prey upon the vulnerable peasant population is unsustainable. It is unsustainable when viewed from above, because the Lord of the covenant will not tolerate such practice. It is unsustainable when viewed from below, because a viable social order cannot endure such exploitative conflict and differential. Thus the theme of prophetic judgment is the declaration that an exploitative economy is unsustainable; it will fail and cause the disruption of social order, social well-being, and social institutions.[4] Specifically, it will cause the loss of wealth among the predators who have ruthlessly taken what belongs to others.

Recall that Solomon's united monarchy was disrupted by the tax revolt of 1 Kings 12:1–19. Moreover, recall that the policies of royal confiscation by the Omri dynasty in the north (Ahab) evoked harsh prophetic judgment against the dynasty (21:21–24). But neither regime seemed to learn from tax revolt or harsh prophetic condemnation. As a result, by the eighth century the economy had developed into an unbearable mismatch between the wealth of the *urban elites* in Samaria and Jerusalem and the *vulnerable agricultural peasants* who were reduced to near subsistence existence. By an appeal to Isaiah 5:8–10, D. N. Premnath terms this economic reductionism a process of "latifundialization" whereby the wealthy bought up increasing amounts of agricultural land, thereby denying the peasant population the capacity to live a viable economic life (see Gen. 47:13–26).[5] The wide and widening economic gap between the haves and have-nots evoked prophetic commentary and protest that declared such economic policy and practice unacceptable and unsustainable. We may cite from three eighth-century prophets:

1. Amos, reckoned to be the earliest of these poets, described the unseemly self-indulgence of the leisure class:

> Alas for those who lie on beds of ivory,
>   and lounge on their couches,
> and eat lambs from the flock,
>   and calves from the stall;
> who sing idle songs to the sound of the harp,
>   and like David improvise on instruments of music;
> who drink wine from bowls,
>   and anoint themselves with the finest oils.
>
> Amos 6:4–6a

The rhetoric smacks of extravagant expenditure of resources for amusement and indulgence. The inventory of lambs, calves, wine, and finest oil suggests a careless consumerism. The critique is that such venal indulgence has narcotized the wealthy to the social implications of their actions: they "are not grieved over the ruin of Joseph" (v. 6b).

They do not have enough good sense to realize that such a style of life will lead to the "ruin" of the community. The extraction of wealth for self-indulgence blinds them to the destructive implications of the practices. The poignant conclusion comes with the prophetic "therefore" in verse 7:

> Therefore they shall now be the first to go into exile,
>   and the revelry of the loungers shall pass away.

The "therefore" is an act of imagination rooted in the logic of deeds-consequences;[6] the poet judges that "revelry" of this kind will result in exile. The prophetic conclusion must have seemed outrageous to those who "innocently" used disproportionate measures of wealth for themselves at the expense of the peasant class that was never given access to such leisure investments. In 8:4–5 Amos describes dishonest commerce—false weights and measures—whereby the poor are cheated in the marketplace. His famous summons to "justice and righteousness" calls attention to the lack of such neighborly actions in an economy that is completely skewed by self-indulgence that has no regard for neighbors who are simply left behind by the privileged with their surplus wealth.

2. Isaiah bears witness to the distorted economy of Jerusalem that had come to be regarded as normal. Jerusalem, the center of the predatory economy, is condemned for its failure to care for all of its population:

> Your princes are rebels
>   and companions of thieves.
> Everyone loves a bribe
>   and runs after gifts.
> They do not defend the orphan,
>   and the widow's cause does not come before them.
>   Isa. 1:23

In a remarkable poem in chapter 2, the poet characterizes the people and the land in their failed practices:

> Indeed they are *full* of diviners from the east
>   and of soothsayers like the Philistines,
>   and they clasp hands with foreigners.
> Their land is *filled* with silver and gold,
>   and there is no end to their treasures;
> their land is *filled* with horses,
>   and there is no end to their chariots.
> Their land is *filled* with idols;
>   they bow down to the work of their hands,
>   to what their own fingers have made.
>   2:6b–8; emphasis added

The fourfold "full" is quite astonishing:

- Full of soothsayers, a reference to predictive capacities to manage and manipulate the socioeconomic scene to certain advantage

by penetrating the "mysteries" of holy power
- Full of silver and gold, surplus wealth extracted from peasants
- Full of horses and chariots, armaments to protect the surplus
- Full of idols, self-constructed commodities of legitimacy

The convergence of wealth, arms, and religious icons permits the construction of a pretend society that is completely cut off from socioeconomic reality.

That social analysis is matched, in what follows in the poem, by the anticipation of the intrusion of the Lord of hosts who will, the poet imagines, move decisively and devastatingly against God's own chosen city. The pounding repetition of "against" situates God as an adversary of the chosen elite who have forfeited their status as the chosen:[7]

> For the LORD of hosts has a day
>   against all that is proud and lofty,
>   against all that is lifted up and high;
> against all the cedars of Lebanon,
>   lofty and lifted up,
>   and against all the oaks of Bashan;
> against all the high mountains,
>   and against all the lofty hills,
> against every high tower,
>   and against every fortified wall;
> against all the ships of Tarshish,
>   and against all the beautiful craft.
>   vv. 12–16

The poetry is not a prediction. It is rather an act of imagination; the poet invites his listeners to imagine the undoing of an economy that has failed to serve the population well and so has failed the intent of YHWH. The poem is an anticipation of the fate of the economy when seen in the purview of divine expectation. As a consequence, the Lord will "take away" all the extravagant consumer goods of the self-indulgent, socially indifferent elite (3:1, 18–23).

The dark side of such consumerism, inevitably, is the abuse of the poor, for the economy is misdirected away from its proper function:

> The LORD enters into judgment
>   with the elders and princes of his people:

It is you who have devoured the vineyard;
   the spoil of the poor is in your houses.
What do you mean by crushing my people,
   by grinding the face of the poor? says the Lord GOD of hosts.

vv. 14–15

The poet offers a series of woes, the final one of which is voiced in 10:1–4:

Ah, you who make iniquitous decrees,
   who write oppressive statutes,
to turn aside the needy from justice
   and to rob the poor of my people of their right,
that widows may be your spoil,
   and that you may make the orphans your prey!
What will you do on the day of punishment,
   in the calamity that will come from far away?
To whom will you flee for help,
   and where will you leave your wealth,
so as not to crouch among the prisoners
   or fall among the slain?
For all this his anger has not turned away;
   his hand is stretched out still.

The abuse of the needy poor is accomplished by legislation. The practice of greed is not simply in common consumer practice, but in arrangements of loans, interest, credit, mortgages, and taxes. It is this that "robs" the poor. The poet anticipates "calamity" that will come and cause flight that will entail the abandonment of wealth. You cannot take it with you, not only when you die, but also when you must flee for your life and travel light in the face of terror. The poet can imagine the erstwhile wealthy hiding in caves and holes when the threat comes (2:19–21). In such circumstance of unspeakable danger, "idols of silver" and "idols of gold" will be of no value. In an instant all the accumulated commodities will be worthless, and those who have accumulated them will be in jeopardy. The real threats are quite this-worldly in terms of military invasion. In poetry, however, the coming threat is from the holy God who finds the predatory economy unbearable—and will terminate it!

3. The prophet Micah offers two poetic units that imagine the total collapse of the regime that is dependent upon rapacious economic practices. In Micah 2:1–2 the poet connects economic practice directly to the tenth commandment, on coveting:

> Alas for those who devise wickedness
> and evil deeds on their beds!
> When the morning dawns, they perform it,
> because it is in their power.
> They covet fields, and seize them;
> houses, and take them away;
> they oppress householder and house,
> people and their inheritance.

Powerful economic interests buy up and occupy the land of vulnerable peasants. In the next chapter, Micah characterizes the socioeconomic arrangements whereby the powerful—ruler, prophet, priest—collude in economic exploitation (3:9–11a). They do so on the assumption that as God's chosen people, all will be well. They imagine that chosenness gives a free permit to operate a regime of exploitative injustice:

> Yet they lean upon the LORD and say,
> "Surely the LORD is with us!
> No harm shall come upon us."
> v. 11b

The poet, however, knows otherwise and issues a mighty "therefore":

> Therefore because of you
> Zion shall be plowed as a field;
> Jerusalem shall become a heap of ruins,
> and the mountain of the house a wooded height.
> v. 12

Micah can envision a coming time when proud Jerusalem, in all its Solomonic splendor, will be razed to the ground. Micah has no need to mention the coming Assyrian army. That is all to be inferred. But his listeners could not have missed the point. In this perspective, the prosperous economy of the elites was a bubble soon to burst.

III

The matter has grown only more acute by the seventh century. Now the threat has morphed from Assyria to Babylon, but the crisis continues unabated. It is as though the practitioners of greedy exploitation are unable to change and so are fated to demise. We cite three prophets from the final days of the Jerusalem establishment:

1. Jeremiah was the prophet most acutely engaged with the issue of failure to obey Torah. The Deuteronomic "if" that states the condition of obedience to Torah figures in Jeremiah's judgment upon Jerusalem:[8]

> If you truly amend your ways and your doings, if you truly act justly one with another, if you do not oppress the alien, the orphan, and the widow, or shed innocent blood in this place, and if you do not go after other gods to your own hurt, then I will dwell with you in this place, in the land that I gave of old to your ancestors forever and ever. (Jer 7:5–7)

In the next verses Jeremiah refers directly to the Decalogue and anticipates that disobedience will lead to displacement:

> Here you are, trusting in deceptive words to no avail. Will you steal, murder, commit adultery, swear falsely, make offerings to Baal, and go after other gods that you have not known, and then come and stand before me in this house, which is called by my name, and say, "We are safe!"—only to go on doing all these abominations? . . . [T]herefore I will do to the house that is called by my name, in which you trust, and to the place that I gave to you and to your ancestors, just what I did to Shiloh. And I will cast you out of my sight, just as I cast out all your kinsfolk, all the offspring of Ephraim. (vv. 8–10, 14–15)

That prose analysis is given poetic articulation in 5:26–28:

> For scoundrels are found among my people;
>   they take over the goods of others.
> Like fowlers they set a trap;
>   they catch human beings.
> Like a cage full of birds,
>   their houses are full of treachery;

therefore they have become great and rich,
    they have grown fat and sleek.
They know no limits in deeds of wickedness;
    they do not judge with justice
the cause of the orphan, to make it prosper,
    and they do not defend the rights of the needy.

The term rendered "scoundrel" is *rasha'*, the "wicked" or the "guilty," that is, those who violate Torah and disrupt the common good. Their actions consist in confiscation, so that they "trap" human beings the way birds are trapped. And because of such actions, they have become "great and rich," "fat and sleek." The indictment concerns "foolish senseless people" (v. 21) who do not fear God (v. 24), who imagine they are free to do what they want. What they want (and must have!), moreover, is the control of a skewed economy so that vulnerable people are reduced to captured commodities. Thus the scoundrels are not outlaws, rogues; rather, they are those who manipulate the economy in devious ways to their own advantage. The poet has no doubt that their great wealth is a result of their treacherous exploitation of those caught in their economic manipulations like helpless birds in a cage. It is wealth secured at the expense of the community!

Because the scoundrels (the guilty!) have no restraint, the inevitable outcome of their practices is injustice toward orphans and the needy whose legitimate rights in the economy are disregarded. It could have been otherwise. These same powerful people could have managed the economy to cause the vulnerable to prosper. But they did not, and so they are ready candidates for retributive punishment. The argument is an appeal to Torah justice; but the specificity of the argument concerns the suffering of the vulnerable.

The failed king is indicted in the poetry of Jeremiah 22:13–15:

Woe to him who builds his house by unrighteousness,
    and his upper rooms by injustice;
who makes his neighbors work for nothing,
    and does not give them their wages;
who says, "I will build myself a spacious house
    with large upper rooms,"
and who cuts out windows for it,

> paneling it with cedar,
>   and painting it with vermilion.
> Are you a king
>   because you compete in cedar?

The woe pronounced against the king indicates that huge trouble is coming upon king and city. The indictment concerns *unrighteousness* and *injustice*, that is, the failure to enhance the common good for all the people of the realm. On the one hand, the king is guilty of economic extravagance in the form of large upper rooms, windows, and cedar paneling. On the other hand, the indictment concerns failure to pay workers; the self-indulgent showiness of the royal enterprise depends upon cheap labor. Adequate responsible governance, by contrast, is the practice of justice and righteousness for the poor, a practice credited here to Josiah, the father of the king. The king is a shabby contrast to his good father:

> But your eyes and heart
>   are only on your dishonest gain,
> for shedding innocent blood,
>   and for practicing oppression and violence.
>
> v. 17

In poetic idiom the prophet does a shrewd economic analysis and knows very well that low wages for cheap labor cannot be the basis for a viable society. Like so much of Jeremiah, these verses have an acute ring of contemporaneity for us, as we struggle in the midst of huge concentrations of wealth to raise the minimum wage. The old and recurring temptation to ground *prosperity for some* in *the cheap labor of others* is enough, says the poet, to bring enormous woe on the city.

2. The themes of Jeremiah are echoed by Habakkuk. It is astonishing that in the long history of Christian theology, Habakkuk 2:4 has been prominent because it highlights "the righteous [who] live by their faith," but no notice has been taken of the very next verse:

> Moreover, wealth is treacherous;
>   the arrogant do not endure.
> They open their throats as wide as Sheol;
>   like Death they never have enough.

They gather all nations for themselves,
and collect all peoples as their own.

v. 5

The verse concerns trust in wealth rather than reliance on the vision noted in the preceding verses:

> If the fainthearted person does not trust the vision, if he considers it unreliable and thus refuses to walk in it, how much more will wealth prove deceitful to the one who seeks life by pursuing it? The arrogant man who reaches for wealth and power with insatiable, unbridled lust will not reach his goal. Thus the reliability of the vision is set over against the deceitfulness of wealth and power.[9]

It is mind-boggling to think how different the history of theology might have been if the Reformation accent on verse 4 had been connected to the substance of verse 5.

It is, moreover, no wonder that verse 5 is followed by a series of woes in verses 6–19 that detail the sure outcome of reliance on "treacherous" wealth:

- Big trouble to come on those who "heap up" what is not their own. The language concerns pledge (collateral), credit, booty, and plunder, culminating in violence (vv. 6–8).
- Big trouble to come on those who acquire "evil gain" (v. 9) or "gain by violence"
- Big trouble to come on a town (Jerusalem in context?) built "by bloodshed," that is, by exploitative economic practices (v. 12)

The series of woes makes clear that public policy and practice not grounded in faith, not implemented by "the righteous," will lead to disaster. The continuing capacity of Christian interpretation to separate the theology of verse 4 from the materiality of verses 5–19 is an indication of how poorly the tradition has engaged the crucial economic dimension of the horizon of faith.

3. Because the prophet Ezekiel is a priest who is occupied with the holiness and glory of God, we may not at the outset expect him to be concerned with economic questions. But of course, the temple was very much an economic institution that was powerfully at work

in the adjudication of money and possessions. We may notice two quite remarkable passages in which this priestly voice attends to the economy. In Ezekiel 18:5–18, the prophet traces three generations of "a man," likely a king. In all three cases—the righteous man (vv. 5–9), the unrighteous son (vv. 10–14), and the righteous grandson (vv. 14–18)—the prophet enumerates the three defining acts of righteousness.[10] First there is idolatry; second, sexual affront; third, economics:

> . . . does not oppress anyone, but restores to the debtor his pledge, commits no robbery, gives his bread to the hungry and covers the naked with a garment, does not take advance or accrued interest, withholds his hand from iniquity, executes true justice between contending parties . . . (vv. 7–8)

> . . . oppresses the poor and needy, commits robbery, does not restore the pledge, lifts up his eyes to the idols, commits abomination, takes advance or accrued interest . . . (vv. 12–13)

> . . . does not wrong anyone, exacts no pledge, commits no robbery, but gives his bread to the hungry and covers the naked with a garment, withholds his hand from iniquity, takes no advance or accrued interest . . . (vv. 16–17)

It is respect for and justice toward the neighbor in economic matters that receives the fullest exposition in each of the three cases; economic practice becomes one of the defining norms of life-giving righteousness. These three statements contain a surprising element of specificity about how wealth is managed equitably or not. Such equity in economics is decisive for the life of the righteous-innocent and the death of the wicked-guilty.

Perhaps most surprising of all is the indictment of Jerusalem in the long recital of chapter 16, in which the city is treated under the metaphor of Sodom. Given Ezekiel's preoccupation with "abomination" and his utilization of sexuality in a metaphorical way, we might expect Sodom would be indicted for sexual misconduct.[11] In fact, however, the guilt of Sodom is economic extravagance at the expense of the poor and needy: "This was the guilt of your sister Sodom: she and her daughters had pride, excess of food, and prosperous ease, but did not aid the poor and needy" (16:49).

It is this, says the prophet, that amounts to an abomination and that results in "removal." Given all the adrenaline used in the church on issues of sexuality, it is astonishing that we have not considered the economic sin of Sodom. Such neglect suggests the willful refusal of the church to recognize the centrality of economy in the practice of fidelity and the Bible's vision of salvation.

IV

The rhetoric of the prophets in the sixth century after the destruction of Jerusalem continues to be concerned with matters of indictment and sentence for those who have violated Torah and sought to muster a life of prosperity through autonomy. Only now the rhetoric has been redirected; it no longer concerns Israel, who has been defeated. Now it addresses the arrogance of the nations who in their military success and economic prosperity imagine that they are self-sufficient and guaranteed to perpetuity. Their great affront, as Donald Gowan has noted, is their arrogance, which fails to recognize the limits on grandeur that are imposed by the reality of YHWH: "*Hybris* as we have defined its Old Testament sense is full rebellion against God; the effort to take control of the world and all of life and to do without any God but oneself."[12]

In the face of such imperial arrogance, the rhetoric of the prophets comes like a voice from elsewhere. Claiming to be rooted in the authority of YHWH the creator, the rhetoric breaks in upon the totalism of empire and anticipates the collapse and demise of empires in a way that is of course beneficial to Israel. Among the several dimensions of such demise, loss of ill-gotten wealth is noted. We may notice that in Isaiah 47:6 Babylon is condemned because it "showed no mercy." The entire covenantal-prophetic tradition is committed to the notion that mercy willed by YHWH sets a limit on predatory wealth. In the preexilic prophets, such mercy is toward the poor and needy. In the exilic texts, such mercy is toward vulnerable Israel. In both cases, mercy willed by YHWH precludes the seizure of wealth and the limitless, unrestrained practice of power. Such desire for wealth, say the prophets, is insatiable. Thus the prophetic word intrudes into regimes of self-sufficiency:

1. Jeremiah anticipates the demise of Babylon's predatory wealth:

Come against her from every quarter;
  open her granaries;
pile her up like heaps of grain, and destroy her utterly;
  let nothing be left of her.
Kill all her bulls,
  let them go down to the slaughter.
Alas for them, their day has come,
  the time of their punishment!
                              Jer. 50:26–27

"King Nebuchadnezzar . . . has filled his belly with my
  delicacies. . . ."
and Babylon shall become a heap of ruins,
  a den of jackals,
an object of horror and of hissing,
  without inhabitant.
                              51:34, 37

2. Isaiah anticipates the complete reversal of Babylon from noble
ruler to vulnerable slave:

Come down and sit in the dust,
  virgin daughter Babylon!
Sit on the ground without a throne,
  daughter Chaldea!
For you shall no more be called
  tender and delicate.
Take the millstone and grind meal,
  remove your veil,
strip off your robe, uncover your legs,
  pass through the rivers.
Your nakedness shall be uncovered,
  and your shame shall be seen.
                              Isa. 47:1–3

Like every such empire, Babylon had attached its religious passion to silver and gold:

Those who lavish gold from the purse,
  and weigh out silver in the scales—

they hire a goldsmith, who makes it into a god;
    then they fall down and worship!
They lift it to their shoulders, they carry it,
    they set it in its place, and it stands there;
    it cannot move from its place.
If one cries to it, it does not answer
    or save anyone from trouble.

46:6–7

The gods of silver and gold never mandate mercy. But of course such gods cannot save. The regime that has chosen gold and silver to the neglect of mercy, a "lover of pleasures," cannot be sustained:

Now therefore hear this, you lover of pleasures,
    who sit securely,
who say in your heart,
    "I am, and there is no one besides me;
I shall not sit as a widow
    or know the loss of children"—
both these things shall come upon you
    in a moment, in one day;
the loss of children and widowhood
    shall come upon you in full measure,
in spite of your many sorceries
    and the great power of your enchantments.

47:8–9

3. Ezekiel can imagine the loss of wealth in Tyre, emblem of the great commercial city:

Your riches, your wares, your merchandise,
    your mariners and your pilots,
your caulkers, your dealers in merchandise,
    and all your warriors within you,
with all the company
    that is with you,
sink into the heart of the seas
    on the day of your ruin.

Ezek. 27:27[13]

You were in Eden, the garden of God;
    every precious stone was your covering,

carnelian, chrysolite, and moonstone,
    beryl, onyx, and jasper,
sapphire, turquoise, and emerald;
    and worked in gold were your settings
    and your engravings. . . .
In the abundance of your trade
    you were filled with violence, and you sinned;
so I cast you as a profane thing from the mountain of God,
    and the guardian cherub drove you out
    from among the stones of fire. . . .
By the multitude of your iniquities,
    in the unrighteousness of your trade,
    you profaned your sanctuaries.
So I brought out fire from within you;
    it consumed you,
and I turned you to ashes on the earth
    in the sight of all who saw you.

28:13, 16, 18

The future would, moreover, not be different for Egypt, which also stands under the threat of coming judgment (see 30:4). In any place, arrogance that manages wealth against the common good will lead to loss!

V

Both the eighth- and seventh-century prophets in Israel-Judah and the sixth-century prophets concerned with empires were vindicated by historical outcomes. The regimes of greedy confiscation did come to an end. Such regimes regularly turned out to be unsustainable, whether in Jerusalem or Nineveh or Babylon or Tyre. The old covenantal connection between *Torah obedience* and *prosperity* was true, even for regimes that knew nothing of Israel's Torah. The intrusive prophetic voices that regimes wanted to silence turned out to be truth-tellers.

But, as we see in the next chapter, there is more truth to be told! It is not often enough recognized that prophetic speech and therefore prophetic ministry is not fully defined by such warning, indictment, and anticipated demise. The canonical structure of the prophetic books provides that before they finish, the prophets segue to new possibility beyond demise and abyss. That new possibility comes as divine promise, as a resolve for salvation.[14] It is a promise that summons to ecstatic hope. One dimension of a promised future of well-being is the gift of new economic resources that will be completely in contrast to the present failed condition of despair and vulnerability. Prophetic salvation concerns restoration of material well-being in the concrete sphere of lived history or, as we say, "on earth as it is in heaven."

Questions for Reflection

1. For us to imagine and work to achieve a world free from oppression and economic abuse, we must first become aware of how those systems of oppression are established. One of those ways, just as in antiquity, is through legislation. Look at local, state, and federal laws. Which of these laws abuse those who experience poverty? Which of these laws are driven by greed and power?

2. Removal and displacement of the unjust and unrighteous is often described in the prophets as part of the consequence of going against the Torah and the good of the community. This "removal" of the unrighteous has often been misused to target our siblings in LGBTQIA+ communities as well as other marginalized groups. Why do you think that churches or individuals tend to overlook or ignore the principle of economic righteousness? Why do you think we have skewed what it means to be "righteous" or "just" in order to create abusive and dehumanizing rules around moral or racial purity?

3. Regimes that do not uphold the common good—that are solely focused on greed and wealth, consumption and production—tend to fall. Where do you see this kind of disintegration happening in our current society? What do you hope will arise in its place?

4. The prophets spoke in creative poetry and prose in order to help their readers and listeners absorb their messages of justice and righteousness. Try writing your own short piece of prose, or a poem or song. What message do you want to convey? What does your community need to hear?

Chapter 11

Prophetic Hope

A Vision of Economic Liberation and Inclusivity

As we have seen in the previous chapter, the prophets voiced stringent judgments with powerful, disruptive force. Their poetic oracles targeted the royal regimes in Israel and Judah and, subsequently, the imperial regimes in Babylonia and Persia that were committed to economic extraction of wealth from laborers to support nonproductive, governing elites. Yet prophets do not only utter indictments anticipating the demise of exploitative regimes. The emancipatory imagination of prophetic books segues to new possibilities, offered as divine promises with a resolve for salvific restoration. This prophetic promise summons readers to ecstatic hope beyond the abyss of judgment.

I

We may recognize that both the *stringent judgments* and the *ecstatic anticipations* voiced by the prophets are cast as poetry. They are verbal (or written, in the case of Ezekiel) declarations that intend to contradict the world that is immediately in front of the listening community. Thus the *poetry of judgment* contradicts the congratulatory self-sufficiency, in turn, of Jerusalem and of the empires. That poetry asserts that unjust wealth cannot be sustained. The *promissory poetry* contradicts the despair of centralized extraction and asserts that such policy and practice will, soon or late, yield to the resolve of YHWH. It is all poetry. This emancipated rhetoric refuses establishment restraint and dares to link the material reality of life to the rule of YHWH, the very resolve that moneyed interests characteristically want to dismiss as fantasy.

These superb acts of imagination, in the traditioning process, have been woven into a sustained counternarrative that runs against the dominant narrative of the Jerusalem elite or the dominant narrative of empire. This counternarrative refuses the obdurate *denial* of preexilic Jerusalem and imagines the inescapable failure of an economy of extraction. The counternarrative refuses, in like manner, the *despair* of the exilic community that could see no way out of the imperial grip.[1] This counternarrative thus pivots on the *loss* of ill-gotten, ill-managed wealth and on the *restoration* of wealth that will fund the abundant life intended by the God of Israel. These two accents on *loss and restoration* defy monetary realism, a defiance legitimated, in poetic discourse, by the God who wills and presides over an alternative economy.

In reading such a sustained act of imagination, we do not fully understand how the several poetic pieces, likely delivered in an ad hoc and random way, were woven into a coherent communal, canonical vision. Nor do we know how it was that these several poetic traditions could turn abruptly from the *poetry of loss* to the *poetry of possibility*. We can only observe that the poetry did become canon. We can see, moreover, that the *imagination of loss* was indeed transposed into the *imagination of restoration*. These two interpretive maneuvers are defining for the prophetic corpus. They may reflect shrewd discernment rooted in a deeply held ideology that refused the facts on the ground; or they may be the fruit of the Spirit who blows where it will. Or perhaps it is both! Whether *ideological courage* or *Spirit-led conviction*, or both, the outcome is a way to live differently in the world. Worship of this God is more than sacrifice that so easily became in Israel (as elsewhere) an act of commodity bargaining. Life in this covenant is more than commodity:

> For I desire steadfast love and not sacrifice,
>   the knowledge of God rather than burnt offerings.
>   Hos. 6:6

Something decisive happens to wealth and possessions when they are held closely in the sphere of steadfast love and knowledge of God.

II

The theme of restored wealth and well-being is recurrent in the latter prophetic books; see Isaiah 54:11–13; Jeremiah 31:12; Ezekiel 34:13–14; 36:29; Haggai 2:7–9; Zechariah 14:14. The wealth promised to restored Israel is to be given to the faithful remnant that intends full Torah obedience. Thus, while the new wealth is freely given by God (confiscated from the nations), it is to be given to a community of obedience.

The fullest, most important articulation of this future possibility guaranteed by divine promise is in the exultant poetry of Isaiah 60–62. These chapters promise a full and glorious restoration of Jerusalem as the site of YHWH's presence and as the restored home of the Jewish remnant. We may in particular notice two remarkable statements about the coming economy of Jerusalem. The poet imagines a great procession home, once Israel has been freed from Babylonian restraint. The procession will include sons and daughters, all heirs to the promise! Beyond that it will include abundance carried by a caravan of camels laden with precious metals, followed by flocks and herds, all signifiers of wealth in that ancient economy:

> Lift up your eyes and look around;
>> they shall gather together, they come to you;
> your sons shall come from far away,
>> and your daughters shall be carried on their nurses' arms.
> Then you shall see and be radiant;
>> your heart shall thrill and rejoice,
> because the abundance of the sea shall be brought to you,
>> the wealth of the nations shall come to you.
> A multitude of camels shall cover you,
>> the young camels of Midian and Ephah;
>> all those from Sheba shall come.
> They shall bring gold and frankincense,
>> and shall proclaim the praise of the LORD.
> All the flocks of Kedar shall be gathered to you,
>> the rams of Nebaioth shall minister to you;
> they shall be acceptable on my altar,
>> and I will glorify my glorious house.
>
> 60:4–7

This is to be a showy procession! No reason for such abundance is voiced. No condition is stipulated. The destruction of Jerusalem had featured the confiscation of Jerusalem's wealth by military procedure. Now the process is reversed. Jerusalem will become a busy venue for commerce, so that trading centers and ports of entry will operate 24/7 to receive the lavish wealth that will pour in:

> For the coastlands shall wait for me,
>> the ships of Tarshish first,
> to bring your children from far away,
>> their silver and gold with them,
> for the name of the LORD your God,
>> and for the Holy One of Israel,
>> because he has glorified you.
> Foreigners shall build up your walls,
>> and their kings shall minister to you;
> for in my wrath I struck you down,
>> but in my favor I have had mercy on you.
> Your gates shall always be open;
>> day and night they shall not be shut,
> so that nations shall bring you their wealth,
>> with their kings led in procession.
>> vv. 9–11

The reference to the "ships of Tarshish" in verse 9 is likely an allusion to Tarshish in 2:16. The two references together are typical of the book of Isaiah, which can take an image of judgment in the early part of the book and retrieve it as a sign of hope in the latter part. Thus in Isaiah 2 the ships of Tarshish signify arrogance; in chapter 60 these same ships concern the great wealth to be given to Jerusalem.

The imagery in 61:5–6 anticipates a renewal as the community that has been shamed before the nations now will be glorified and honored by the nations; "foreigners" and "strangers" will be cast as menial labor to free Israel for priestly performance and for the sheer enjoyment of wealth. More than a restitution of what was lost, now their wealth will be a "double portion," signifying the splendor of Jerusalem and the temple:

> Strangers shall stand and feed your flocks,
>> foreigners shall till your land and dress your vines;

but you shall be called priests of the LORD,
    you shall be named ministers of our God;
you shall enjoy the wealth of the nations,
    and in their riches you shall glory.
Because their shame was double,
    and dishonor was proclaimed as their lot,
therefore they shall possess a double portion;
    everlasting joy shall be theirs.

61:5–7[2]

It is all gift! It is all unearned wealth! The recovery is deeply rooted in fidelity on God's part; it is manifested fully and without embarrassment or explanation materially!

III

At least two vexing questions trouble such soaring poetry of promise. On the one hand, we may briefly note the tension between such soaring promises of renewal and the much more sober historical realities underlying the poetry. Israel's greatest voice of hope, Second Isaiah, sounded precisely amid a community of displaced people (Isa. 40–55). It is the truth of biblical faith that the God of hope is most powerfully present in seasons of hopelessness. Thus, the poetry of the book of Lamentations, a near contemporary of Second Isaiah, concedes:

Gone is my glory, and all that I had hoped for from the LORD.
Lam. 3:18[3]

Out of that moment of grief and loss in the exile, Second Isaiah imagined a wondrous homecoming and restoration to Jerusalem.

We pick up the story just at the edge of the city as the returning exiles moved from hope to a historical reality that is much more modest than the hope of Second Isaiah. I take up these texts because all of us must think of the future of God's people. Like those ancients, we too now have great evangelical promises ringing in our ears, even while we face the vexed reality of the facts on the ground. Poised between hope and reality, perhaps we also vacillate, as did they, thinking variously that this is an impossible moment of difficulty or that this is a wondrous moment of possibility. The returning exiles did not know the future as they arrived back in town . . . and we do not know either.

The other troubling question relating to the prophetic pronouncements of restoration regards inclusion. Who will participate in this gloriously restored future? Alternatively, who will be excluded from the community that strives for and awaits such restoration?

These questions begin already with Israel's founding, paradigmatic story of emancipation. The formation of Israel is narrated as a process whereby YHWH's power transformed "no people" into "this people":

- The Hebrews, as forerunners of Israel, were treated, according to the tradition, as marginal, objectionable people. Indeed, in the Joseph narrative they were regarded as a threat to social propriety and kept separated from those who managed social power:

  They served him by himself, and them by themselves, and the Egyptians who ate with him by themselves, because the Egyptians could not eat with the Hebrews, for that is an abomination to the Egyptians. (Gen. 43:32)

That treatment is not unlike the way in which whites have characteristically treated Blacks in U.S. society.

In the exodus narrative it is remembered that Israel, in its departure from Egypt, was a "mixed multitude," not a readily identified population (Exod. 12:38).

At Sinai, however, this gathering of disparate populations was formed and transformed by the will of YHWH into an identifiable, intentional community, called to a historical destiny (Exod. 19:5–6). The wonder of the people of God in the Old Testament is the marvel of transformation whereby "not a people" became "God's people" (see 1 Pet. 2:10).

Prophetic tradition remembered that transformative miracle of identity. On the one hand, Israel could imagine its becoming, yet again, "not my people" (Hos. 1:9). But, on the other hand, it also trusted divine fidelity to cause them to become, always anew, "my people" (2:23). The identity of Israel as YHWH's people is a treasured claim, but one permeated with risk. For that reason, Israel always contested its identity, its destiny, and, consequently, its membership.

IV

After the wonder of exodus-Sinai and the doxological expression of that wonder, it did not take very long for Israel, in its traditioning process, to try to give order to its life and to establish boundaries of membership, to determine who was in and who was not. In general it is right to say that the "insiders," the legitimate members of this community of YHWH, are those who keep Torah, who obey the commandments of Sinai, and who swear allegiance to these commandments. Joshua 24 presents a liturgical occasion whereby a subsequent generation that was never at Sinai replicated Sinai, reiterated the oath of allegiance, and signed on as Israel:

> He said, "Then put away the foreign gods that are among you, and incline your hearts to the LORD, the God of Israel." The people said to Joshua, "The LORD our God we will serve, and him we will obey." So Joshua made a covenant with the people that day, and made statutes and ordinances for them at Shechem. (Josh. 24:23–25)

It is plausible to imagine that over time Israel reenacted this drama many times, always again incorporating new members into the community of Torah.

That practice of Torah whereby Israel received and sustained its identity as the people of YHWH is expressed in the two great interpretive traditions of Torah. First, there is the great Priestly tradition of holiness, voiced in the book of Leviticus, that summoned Israel to be a holy people:

> Speak to all the congregation of the people of Israel and say to them: You shall be holy, for I the LORD your God am holy. (Lev. 19:2)

That tradition calls Israel to cultic purity, to stay clear of all that is profane and worldly, and common, because such exposures would contaminate Israel and drive YHWH out of Israel's presence. The book of Leviticus, in careful detail, provides guidelines for every phase of life to be sure that membership in Israel consists only in those who sustain intentional purity. Others are excluded because they jeopardize the entire community.

The second great interpretive tradition, Deuteronomy, takes the Sinai commandments in a somewhat different direction. As in the Priestly tradition, purity remains a continuing concern (Deut. 14:1–21), yet Deuteronomy places accent on justice questions and is preoccupied with the vulnerable who need protection by the community: the poor, alongside widows, orphans, and immigrants. Israel consists in those who practice such protective justice (Deut. 16:19–20).

The most interesting text in Deuteronomy on "membership" is the list of exclusions that Moses declares in Deuteronomy 23:1–8. The text is divided into two parts. First, in verses 1–2, Moses excludes from membership those with distorted genitalia, as though proper functioning of genitalia had become a condition of joining the community. It is likely that the accent on testicles and penises relates to the fruitful transmission of sperm in the maintenance of "the holy seed" (see Ezra 9:2; Neh. 9:2). Alongside that, in verse 2, "those born of an illicit union" are excluded. The two verses enunciate criteria of right sexual relations as precondition of membership.

In the second part of the text, Deut 23:3–8, Moses presents a checklist of non-Israelites. On the one hand, Ammonites and Moabites are unwelcome, with reference to ancient memories in the book of Numbers. Remarkably their peace and prosperity are never to be a concern for Israel. Since peace and prosperity are a cultic gift in that ancient community, they are excluded from Israel's worship and so cannot receive covenant blessing from either God or neighbor.

By contrast, Edomites and Egyptians are to be included in the community, a quite astonishing allowance. Edomites are "kin" ("brothers"), remembered according to the ancient connection to Esau. (Interestingly, in Gen. 19:30–38, Ammon and Moab are also "kin," but that point is not observed here.) Egyptians are welcome on very different grounds, by appeal to Israel's own memory of being outsiders in Egypt. One might conclude that this distinction of those "in" and those "out" is arbitrary, but so Moses declares. (This is not the last time such distinctions would be arbitrary!) It is evident in this passage that "membership" is a most serious matter, freighted with good and bad memories; rigorous conditions must be met in order to gain admission to the community.

V

These traditions that regulate membership in Israel through the maintenance of purity, the practice of neighborliness, and adherence to Torah provide a milieu for understanding later prophetic developments regarding this vexed issue of inclusion. The exiles may have departed Babylon dancing to the lyrics of Second Isaiah (Isa. 40–55) with eager longing, but when they arrived at the imagined home city, they did not find king or temple or walls or economy. They found shambles and so they, like their Babylonian counterparts, sat down and wept (Ps. 137:1; Neh. 1:4). Their grief was not yet finished. Then, having wept, they moved into the script of Isaiah 56–66, that is, Third Isaiah.

The big surprise in Third Isaiah is that the community is addressed by urgent imperatives to act. This is a contrast to the lyrics of Isaiah 40–55, which are fundamentally indicative assurance. The move from the *indicative* to the *imperative* is what happens when displaced folks reenter and reengage the failed urban fabric. As they departed on the poet's highway home, they could not simply come home, fit in, and settle. There was nothing left of the infrastructure into which to fit. So they are summoned by this poetry to the hard work of reconstruction. From Isaiah 56–66 I make an interpretive connection to our own time and place of evangelical obedience in a failed urban economy. There will not be, as there was not then, any "return to normalcy," as Hananiah had anticipated (Jer. 28:3–4). What is required now is initiative-taking actions, local and public, that create anew the capacity to sustain human community and the parallel capacity to maintain an ecosystem that honors all of creation. Of course, we cannot, as they did not, know ahead of time what is required. What we do know and can see in this text is that hard thought and resolved work are required out beyond our comfort zone. I recognize, moreover, that as we take Isaiah 56–66 as our guide, other texts and other perspectives urged otherwise.[4] But for now I will consider only this text.

Third Isaiah begins in 56:1–2, with what Rolf Rendtorff suggests is a theme or mantra for the whole:[5]

> Thus says the LORD:
> Maintain justice, and do what is right,
> for soon my salvation will come,
>   and my deliverance be revealed.
> Happy is the mortal who does this,
>   the one who holds it fast,
> who keeps the sabbath, not profaning it,
>   and refrains from doing any evil.

The first words are imperatives: maintain justice, do right. The phrasing looks back to Isaiah 1:21–26. In that opener the poet remembers how Jerusalem was at the beginning:

> How the faithful city
>   has become a whore!
>   She that was full of *justice*,
> *righteousness* lodged in her—
>   but now murderers!
>   Isa. 1:21, emphasis added

And the poet awaits an "afterward" for the city:

> And I will restore your judges as at the first,
>   and your counselors as at the beginning.
> *Afterward* you shall be called the city of *righteousness*,
>   the *faithful* city.
>   v. 26, emphasis added

Our verses in chapter 56 are the "afterward" of reconstruction. The imperative is based on an assurance of divine deliverance. The first step on the way to the new city of justice and right is the generic summons to shun evil and the single covenantal reference to Sabbath. I have come to think that, for those of us inured to empire, Sabbath rest is the most urgent and difficult command, because empires depend upon restless productivity. The mandate that begins the poetry is to disengage.

The community had a number of difficult issues to negotiate, but no issue was more urgent than that of membership. Among the questions to be faced was the matter of admission of Jews to the worship community, those who had been deported and those who had not been deported, those who had cooperated with imperial authorities and those who had not cooperated. It is probable that Isaiah 56:3–8 reflects only one side of this urgently disputed matter, but it is the text we will consider here.

The text is one that startles us because it sets out to contradict and overthrow the ancient rules of Moses in Deuteronomy 23:1–8 by asserting a principle of *inclusiveness* against that ancient *exclusivism*. This poetic assertion advocates the option of including two groups of applicants for membership in Israel. First, welcome the *foreigners*!

> Do not let the foreigner joined to the LORD say,
>> "The LORD will surely separate me from his people"; . . .
> And the foreigners who join themselves to the LORD,
>> to minister to him, to love the name of the LORD,
>> and to be his servants,
> all who keep the sabbath, and do not profane it.
>
> Isa. 56:3a, 6

Second, admit *eunuchs*!

> [A]nd do not let the eunuch say,
>> "I am just a dry tree."
> For thus says the LORD:
> To the eunuchs who keep my sabbaths,
>> who choose the things that please me
>> and hold fast my covenant,
> I will give, in my house and within my walls,
>> a monument and a name
>> better than sons and daughters;
> I will give them an everlasting name
>> that shall not be cut off.
>
> vv. 3b–5

The admission of foreigners clearly contradicts the exclusion of Moabites and Ammonites in Deuteronomy 23 and seems to make it easier for Egyptians as well. It is remarkable that the advocacy of the poem is not deterred by the Torah of Moses. The stance is one of generous inclusiveness.

The admission of eunuchs, even though with different wording, would seem to be intentionally aimed at 23:1, for eunuchs have "compromised" genitalia. Now it may be that the term should not be translated "eunuch," but in any case it would seem to refer to those who had cooperated with and submitted to foreign rulers and thus compromised politically, even if not with reference to genitals.[6] But the more common translation of "eunuchs" can be taken provisionally here as reference to the latter as well. Both categories of applicants are to be made welcome; a picture is presented of a community of faith that is generously expansive and welcoming, quite unlike the initial prescription of Moses.

Most remarkably, the conditions of admission clearly do not concern ethnic qualification or any other criterion of purity. On the one hand, there is the quite generic requirement of the new recruit simply to "keep Torah." That is all. This likely means the Torah of Deuteronomy, but it is not spelled out. Most spectacularly, there is only one condition spelled out: keep Sabbath! This is the single, solitary mark of membership, an act of generous incorporation that outruns the inventory of Moses and that lets the life of God's Israel spill over among those who have been excluded but are now to be welcomed.

How astonishing that of all the conditions for entry into the community the party of inclusiveness might have selected, they opted for Sabbath! They made Sabbath the single specific requirement for membership. That is because Sabbath represents a radical disengagement from the producer-consumer rat race of the empire. The community welcomes members of any race or nation, any gender or social condition, so long as that person is defined by justice, mercy, and compassion, and not competition, achievement, production, or acquisition. There is no mention of purity, only work stoppage with a neighborly pause for humanness.

"These"—says the text—these foreigners, these eunuchs, these whom Moses would not admit, these Sabbath keepers, these persons of faith who refuse to be defined by cultural expectations, are to be admitted:

> [T]hese [foreigners and eunuchs] I will bring to my holy
>   mountain,
>   and make them joyful in my house of prayer;
> their burnt offerings and their sacrifices

will be accepted on my altar;
for my house shall be called a house of prayer for all peoples.

Isa. 56:7

With accents on neighborliness and Sabbath as alternative practices, the poetry anticipates astonishingly inclusive worship in the Jerusalem temple. Finally, the poetry promises that its inclusive impulse will extend across still further boundaries:

Thus says the Lord GOD,
    who gathers the outcasts of Israel,
I will gather others to them
    besides those already gathered.

v. 8

This is an ancient text that corrects an even more ancient text. And now we read this ancient text in our contemporary moment of deciding. Ours is a time of scattering in fear. We are so fearful that we want to fence the world in order to keep all the others out:

- Some of the church still wants to fence out women.
- We build fences to keep out immigrants (or Palestinians).
- The church in many places fences out gay people.
- The old issue of race is still powerful for fencing.

We have so many requirements that are as old as Moses. But here are only two requirements. The first requires members to hold fast to the covenant, which entails engagement for the material well-being of the community. The second is Sabbath, work stoppage, an ordinance everyone can honor—gay or straight or trans, woman or man or nonbinary, Black or white, "American" or immigrant—anybody can keep it and be gathered to the meeting of all of God's people.

VI

Such emancipatory prophetic hope offers an alternative vision of the people of God that is, for us no less than it was in the Persian period, distinctly countercultural and profoundly subversive. This poetry affirms a genuinely alternative way of being human that exposes conventional culture as not only inadequate but as profoundly anti-human. Dominant culture among us is rightly characterized as technological, therapeutic, military consumerism that touches every aspect of our life, public and personal, religious and secular.

To help us think about the mission of God's people in such circumstance, Isaiah 56 provides an inventory of ways that the church can invite people to alternative humanness. To conclude, I will consider that alternative through the five aspects of our text. The urgency of the alternative is in the deep conviction that evangelical conservatives and evangelical liberals share the conviction that our society, in its main accents, has lost its way and is organized against our God-given, God-led humanness.

a. The *exile* as the true character and venue of our humanness is an alternative to the dominant imagination that we live in a centered, coherent world in which we can establish security on our own terms. It matters greatly if the metaphor of exile, deportation, and displacement is an accurate characterization for the context of ministry. The claim of success and security, so powerful among us, causes us not to notice the cast out and often not to acknowledge our own displacement or anxiety about coming displacement.

b. *Openness to foreigners and eunuchs*, that is, welcome to others who are not like us, is a radical alternative to the ideology of conformity that takes all those not like ourselves to be dangerous and unacceptable deviants. The issue, of course, concerns the otherness of sexuality, but it also concerns the otherness of immigrants and those with alternative social practices. That intolerance of the others among us is even more toxic now that our society in the United States is divided into "red" and "blue," and I fear we are at the edge of red and blue clergy and red and blue parishes. And here is this poet who says, let not the foreigner or the eunuch imagine that they will be excluded or forgotten.

c. The *memory of the exodus* that leads to neighborly generosity is the primary mark of a covenantal society. That memory in practice issues in a subordination of the economy to the social fabric with focal attention to the marginated who are without social access, social power, or social advocacy. The covenant is an assertion of interdependence and an institution of mutuality that flies in the face of acquisitiveness that regards everyone else as a competitor for the same commodity or as a threat to my self-securing. The poem is an act of imagination that allows that social relationships are not necessarily cast in terms of aggressive commodity competition, for there is a more elemental belonging with and for each other that chastens such aggressiveness.

d. The *visible practice of Sabbath rest* that disengages from the pursuit of commodity is an insistent assertion about the nature of being human. The pause for receptivity of holy gifts that are inscrutably given is a break in the rigor of production and consumption. Taking time to be human is a deep contrast to the drivenness of the acquisitive life that is always on the make and that ends in fatigue that has no energy for humane living.

e. The *practice of prayer* that binds us in love to God and in love to neighbor beyond our small claim is the resolve to *live life on terms other than our own.* Such yielding to the largeness of God's rule is a challenge to much of our tribalism, for our conventional tribalism limits the scope of concern and teaches us that to yield is to lose.

The conclusion I draw is that on all five issues Isaiah 56 offers a venue for rethinking and redeciding about our place in the world. It is a rethinking and a redeciding not unlike that of fifth-century Judaism and not unlike the regular subversive work of synagogue and church. The witness of this poem is not commonplace; it is, rather, profoundly countercultural, revolutionary, transformative, and subversive. I suggest that this agenda provides clues to our way to be the church in a culture that is increasingly organized against human reality.

I do not suggest that a simple move from dominant modes of reality to this alternative is an easy or obvious one. Nor do I imagine that many of us, liberal or conservative, are easily ready for such a move. But Isaiah 56 provides enough for us to ponder. From its great vision of ingathering, this poet goes on to give detail and nuance to the coming world that will displace the tired world of dominant culture:

In Isaiah 58 we are given an instruction on true worship:

> Is not this the fast that I choose:
>> to loose the bonds of injustice,
>> to undo the thongs of the yoke,
> to let the oppressed go free,
>> and to break every yoke?
> Is it not to share your bread with the hungry,
>> and bring the homeless poor into your house;

when you see the naked, to cover them,
and not to hide yourself from your own kin?

vv. 6–7

It is promised in three "then" clauses that life will be different as a
consequence of right worship:

Then you shall call, and the LORD will answer;
you shall cry for help, and he will say, Here I am.

v. 9

[T]hen your light shall rise in the darkness
and your gloom be like the noonday.
The LORD will guide you continually,
and satisfy your needs in parched places,
and make your bones strong;
and you shall be like a watered garden,
like a spring of water,
whose waters never fail.

vv. 10b–11

[T]hen you shall take delight in the LORD,
and I will make you ride upon the heights of the earth;
I will feed you with the heritage of your ancestor Jacob,
for the mouth of the LORD has spoken.

v. 14

- In Isaiah 61, it is anticipated that there will be a radical alternative practice of human community:

The spirit of the Lord GOD is upon me,
because the LORD has anointed me;
he has sent me to bring good news to the oppressed,
to bind up the brokenhearted,
to proclaim liberty to the captives,
and release to the prisoners;
to proclaim the year of the LORD's favor,
and the day of vengeance of our God;
to comfort all who mourn.

vv. 1–2

Jesus quotes this text at the synagogue in Luke 4:18–19. The text
imagines a Jubilee year, and Jesus dares to claim,

Today this scripture has been fulfilled in your hearing. (v. 21)

They drive him out of their worship that echoes dominant culture, because they rightly perceive that the Jubilee would undo all dominant modes of social relationships.

- In Isaiah 60, as we saw at the beginning of this chapter, it is anticipated that Jerusalem will become the new center of peace and prosperity, that trade will flourish, and foreigners will bring all their precious cargo for trade. The wealthy visitors will hurry to this Jerusalem center of shalom with gold and frankincense. And because God will situate us anew in a healthy world, it is promised at the end of the chapter:

> Your sun shall no more go down,
>   or your moon withdraw itself;
> for the LORD will be your everlasting light,
>   and your days of mourning shall be ended.
> Your people shall all be righteous;
>   they shall possess the land forever.
> They are the shoot that I planted, the work of my hands,
>   so that I might be glorified.
> The least of them shall become a clan,
>   and the smallest one a mighty nation;
> I am the LORD;
>   in its time I will accomplish it quickly.
>
> vv. 20–22

- In Isaiah 65:17–25, a new world is envisioned that offers human relationships rooted in God's presence:

> I will rejoice in Jerusalem,
>   and delight in my people;
> no more shall the sound of weeping be heard in it,
>   or the cry of distress.
> No more shall there be in it
>   an infant that lives but a few days,
>   or an old person who does not live out a lifetime; . . .
> Before they call I will answer,
>   while they are yet speaking I will hear.
> The wolf and the lamb shall feed together,
>   the lion shall eat straw like the ox;

> but the serpent—its food shall be dust!
> They shall not hurt or destroy
>   on all my holy mountain,
>   says the LORD.
>   vv. 19–20, 24–25

All of that is only imagined. It has not yet been given. But for those deep in denial or despair or cynicism or narcissism about dominant culture, this act of imagination that we do in word and sacrament is a genuine alternative. It is an alternative that lives on the lips of the church. Everything depends on that testimony! And when we engage it again, we are filled with energy and courage and generosity, enough to risk and to resist, and to wait with eager longing.

Questions for Reflection

1. Envision a future in which the world is centered on obedience to God and on our neighbors. What would this new world look like in your immediate context? Write a paragraph or poem describing this new world.

2. Now read this paragraph or poem to yourself three times. How does this vision of the future impact how you feel about what is happening in our world? Amid sickness, death, injustice, and hopelessness, how does this vision of the future affect your spirit?

3. Membership in the Israelite community—who was "in" and who was "out"—underwent many changes, ultimately arriving at one requirement: the observance of the Sabbath, the radical disengagement from the empire. But this opening up of membership took the work of acceptance. Who in your life do you consider to be "in" who was once "out" in your community? Why? What does it take to open up membership in a community?

4. In your current and future experience working for justice, how can you envision yourself moving into alternative, God-led humanness through the five aspects Brueggemann presents for rethinking our place in this world? Meditate on and come up with an example for each: the exile, openness to foreigners and eunuchs, the memory of the exodus, visible practice of Sabbath rest, the practice of prayer.

Chapter 12

The Emancipating Imagination of Jesus

I conclude by carrying my exploration of biblical salvation briefly into the New Testament. The key themes and emphases of biblical salvation we have uncovered run right through the narratives of Jesus and other texts in the New Testament. They do not run exclusively toward the New Testament, for clearly early Judaism (as a companion movement) makes parallel interpretive moves. Yet each aspect of biblical salvation that I have reviewed reaches readily into the New Testament.

It is clear that the basic elements of biblical salvation continued into Jesus' day and, beyond that, even still today. First, the ancient Roman Empire perpetuated only a new permutation of the *kingdom of scarcity* with its propelling *ideology of fear and anxiety* that we initially see in Pharaoh's Egypt. Second, the New Testament Gospels portray Jesus in various ways as an agent capable of *immense acts of generosity* that in turn had the capacity to emancipate people from the reigning system of fear, anxiety, and greed. Third, the now-liberated followers of Jesus are then able to receive new instructions orienting them away from entitlements of the self and toward the work of *the well-being of the neighborhood.*

I

Jesus' main term for the alternative community that he commended and performed was the "kingdom of God." His initial pronouncement, according to the Gospel of Mark, is: "The time is fulfilled, and the kingdom of God has come near; repent, and believe in the good news" (Mark 1:15). This kingdom is a social practice and a set of social relationships that are congruent with the God of the covenantal Torah of ancient Israel. His appeal to a political metaphor ("kingdom") assures that his ministry contradicted the dominant kingdom of Rome. His ministry, conducted in subversive act and disruptive word, concerned the performance of an alternative community and economy willed by God, in defiance of the dominant society and economy that was legitimated by Rome and practiced by those who accepted imperial hegemony with its exploitative protocols.

According to the Gospel of Luke, Jesus offers his inaugural address at the synagogue in Nazareth in the region of Galilee (Luke 4:16–30). As we have seen, in it he reads from Isaiah 61:

> The Spirit of the Lord is upon me,
>> because he has anointed me
>> to bring good news to the poor.
> He has sent me to proclaim release to the captives
>> and recovery of sight to the blind,
>>> to let the oppressed go free,
> to proclaim the year of the Lord's favor.
>
> vv. 18–19

The text imagines a Jubilee year. The "year of the Lord's favor" refers to Jubilee and thus to Leviticus 25. Thus the text announces that the Spirit of God is on the loose with an extreme form of the Sabbath principle, to liberate people from all kinds of debts, to forgive all kinds of liabilities. Of course, reading from that Scripture in the synagogue is unexceptional, until Jesus dares to claim:

> Today this scripture has been fulfilled in your hearing. (Luke 4:21)

That is, the person of Jesus is now the embodiment of Jubilee, of Sabbath writ large. Jesus subverts the entire system of coercion upon which society operates. It is no wonder that the crowd in the synagogue surged against him to drive him out of town. All Pharaohs, ancient and contemporary, recognize the Sabbath (and Jubilee) as profoundly subversive and cannot tolerate such deconstructive action. So it is in terms of public reality, and so in personal reality as well. The oppressive society and the coerced person cannot entertain the year or the day of the Lord's favor.

Yet Jesus offers his alternative, which includes a profound invitation to his disciples to unplug from the anxiety system:

> Therefore I tell you, do not worry about your life, what you will eat or what you will drink, or about your body, what you will wear. Is not life more than food, and the body more than clothing? Look at the birds of the air; they neither sow nor reap nor gather into barns, and yet your heavenly Father feeds them. Are you not of more value than they? And can any of you by worrying add a single hour to your span of life? And why do you worry about clothing? Consider the lilies of the field, how they grow; they neither toil nor spin, yet I tell you, even Solomon in all his glory was not clothed like one of these. But if God so clothes the grass of the field, which is alive today and tomorrow is thrown into the oven, will he not much more clothe you—you of little faith? Therefore do not worry, saying, "What will we eat?" or "What will we drink?" or "What will we wear?" (Matt. 6:25–31)

The birds and the lilies are attestation that creation works! Trust it and live out righteousness, and your "heavenly Father"—the creator—will see to your well-being. Behind the sermon away from anxiety by Jesus is the good word of Moses:

> Six days you shall do your work, but on the seventh day you shall rest, so that your ox and your donkey may have relief, and your homeborn slave and the resident alien may be refreshed. Be attentive to all that I have said to you. Do not invoke the names of other gods; do not let them be heard on your lips. (Exod. 23:12–13)

The "other gods" are agents and occasions of anxiety. But Jesus invites us, by discipline, by resolve, by baptism, by Eucharist, and by passion, to resist such seductions. In so doing we stand alongside the creator in whose image we are made.

The Magnificat of Mary (Luke 1:46–55) announces primary themes that recur in the Gospel of Luke. Her song is an anticipation both of the story of Jesus and his ministry that is to follow, including his announcement of Sabbath rest, and of the story of

the early church in the book of Acts. The song is an echo of the
Song of Hannah (1 Sam. 2:1–10), which anticipates the revolutionary rule of David that is to come in ancient Israel and will effect a
social upheaval:

> The bows of the mighty are broken,
>> but the feeble gird on strength.
> Those who were full have hired themselves out for bread,
>> but those who were hungry are fat with spoil. . . .
> The LORD makes poor and makes rich;
>> he brings low, he also exalts.
> He raises up the poor from the dust;
>> He lifts the needy from the ash heap,
> to make them sit with princes
> and inherit a seat of honor.
>
> vv. 4–5a, 7–8

The theme of Hannah, moreover, is reiterated in Psalm 113:7–8:

> He raises the poor from the dust,
>> and lifts the needy from the ash heap,
> to make them sit with princes,
>> with the princes of his people.

That same accent of social upheaval is now on the lips of Mary:

> He has brought down the powerful from their thrones,
>> and lifted up the lowly;
> he has filled the hungry with good things,
>> and sent the rich away empty.
> He has helped his servant Israel,
>> in remembrance of his mercy,
> according to the promise he made to our ancestors,
>> to Abraham and to his descendants forever.
>
> Luke 1:52–55

The parallels clearly assume a class analysis of the powerful and
the lowly who are, inevitably, the rich and the hungry, respectively.
The Gospel of Luke is, from the outset, good news that both chal-
lenges present economic arrangements and anticipates alternative
arrangements.

II

For the church it is the Eucharist that is the great extravagant drama of the way in which the gospel of abundance overrides the claim of scarcity and invites to the common good. There is no doubt that the church's Eucharist is, among other things, simply a replay of the manna narrative in Exodus. The sacrament, when not administered in coercion and anxiety, is a gesture of divine abundance that breaks the scarcity system. So consider:

- In Mark 6:30–44 Jesus came upon a crowd in a "deserted place." He has compassion on them, for "they were like sheep without a shepherd." The reference to "deserted place" and the lack of a shepherd is intentionally reminiscent of the manna narrative in the wilderness. Thus we are told,

> Jesus *took* five loaves and the two fish,
> Jesus *blessed* them,
> Jesus *broke* the loaves,
> Jesus *gave* them to the people.

The four great verbs of abundance are recited and enacted: "He took, he blessed, he broke, he gave." He fed five thousand people. He committed an overt act of abundance that broke the scarcity of the place—such an abundance that there were twelve baskets of bread left over, more than enough!

- In 8:1–10, in case one missed the narrative in chapter 6, Jesus does it all again. He came to a great crowd that was without anything to eat. He had compassion on them; the disciples wondered about "bread in the desert." Again, he enacted the four great verbs of abundance:

> Jesus *took* seven loaves,
> Jesus *gave* thanks,
> He *broke* the loaves,
> He *gave* the bread to his disciples.

Mark reports that he fed four thousand people—such an abundance! Seven baskets of bread left over—loaves abound!

- After these two feedings, Jesus, the master teacher, invites his disciples to reflect on what they had seen. They are in a boat together. They have forgotten the bread, not remembering that Jesus is in the abundance business. Jesus asks the disciples hard questions to which they make no response:

> Why are you talking about having no bread? Do you still not perceive or understand? Are your hearts hardened? Do you have eyes, and fail to see? Do you have ears, and fail to hear? And do you not remember? (8:17–18)

He wants them to reflect on his work of abundance. But they avoid eye contact and make no response. The disciples are beyond their interpretive capacity, because they do not know what to make of the new abundance caused by Jesus.

The connection between the old narrative of Pharaoh and the present wonder is the phrase "hard hearts." The disciples could not compute the meaning of the abundance of loaves. They were prevented from understanding by their hard hearts. Their hard hearts replicated the hard heart of Pharaoh, who, in his anxiety, had dreamed of famine, even when he had more than enough (Gen. 41:1–32; cf. Exod. 4:21; 8:15, 32; 9:12; 10:1, 20, 27; 11:10; 14:4, 8, 17). That is, Pharaoh dreamed of scarcity, a nightmare that led to his extravagant construction of storehouse cities that depended on cheap, exploited labor. The disciples could not understand the new wave of God-given, abundant loaves until and unless they departed their pharaonic ideology of scarcity. But the totalizing claim of scarcity excluded for them any discernment of the new abundance enacted by Jesus. Indeed, the narrative account of the disciples cannot be fully understood without reference to the old pharaonic obtuseness of hard hearts.

Like a good teacher, Jesus retreats to more concrete-operational questions. He reviews the two feeding miracles and then asks how much bread was left over:

- How many baskets of bread were left over in chapter 6 when I fed five thousand?
- They are eager with an answer: "Twelve."
- How many baskets of bread were left over in chapter 8 when I fed four thousand?
- They are eager with an answer: "Seven!"

The disciples are very good at concrete-operational questions. They know the data, but they have no sense of its significance. And then Jesus speaks in weary exasperation to those who know the data but do not get the point. The narrative concludes with what may be Jesus' saddest verdict:

> Do you not yet understand? (Mark 8:21)

Do you not understand that the ideology of *scarcity* has been broken, overwhelmed by the divine gift of *abundance*? Jesus invites the disciples to understand and engage the new governance of the bread that has been blessed, broken, and given . . . in abundance.

III

It is our propensity, in society and in church, to trust the narrative of scarcity. That is what makes us greedy, and exclusive, and selfish, and coercive. Even the Eucharist can be made into an occasion of scarcity, as though there were not enough for all. Such scarcity leads to exclusion at the Table, even as scarcity leads to exclusion from economic life.

But the narrative of abundance persists among us. Those who sign on and depart the system of anxious scarcity become the history-makers in the neighborhood. These are the ones not exhausted by Sabbath-less production who have enough energy to dream and hope. From dreams and hopes come such neighborly miracles as good health care, good schools, good housing, good care for the earth, and disarmament. The dream subverts Pharaoh's nightmare.

Jesus' offer of emancipating abundance is also present in the Fourth Gospel, in which Jesus declares:

> I came that they may have life, and have it abundantly. (John 10:10)

Unlike the false shepherds, the good shepherd assures protection and well-being for the sheep. The Fourth Gospel also reiterates the feeding miracle whereby Jesus feeds five thousand and has twelve baskets of barley loaves left over:

> When they were satisfied, he told his disciples, "Gather up the fragments left over, so that nothing may be lost." So they gathered

them up, and from the fragments of the five barley loaves, left by
those who had eaten, they filled twelve baskets. (6:12–13)

In his teaching at the well, he promises the woman water that will
end all thirst: "Those who drink of the water that I will give them
will never be thirsty. The water that I will give will become in them
a spring of water gushing up to eternal life" (4:14). The gifts of bread
and water attest to the abundance that Jesus gives. They are, to be
sure, sacramental acts, so these usages in the Fourth Gospel are always
laden with surplus meaning. That, however, does not cause the bread
or water to lose its materiality, so that an economic dimension of abundance is implicit in his words and actions. His promise of abundance is
indeed the performance of a new economy that is "from above."

In chapter 12 of John the extravagance of oil for anointing Jesus
evoked opposition from Judas, who was mindful, so he said, of the
poor. We may see that Judas is portrayed as the antipode of Jesus; he
dismisses the abundance of Jesus. Judas thinks in the categories of
the old economy, in terms of a zero-sum notion about money. Money
used for this will not be available for that. In this case, money used
for precious oil will not be available for the poor. Judas has no sense
that, where Jesus prevails, the old economy of parsimony is not in
effect, because Jesus' capacity for abundance is generative of all that
is needed. In the narratives of Matthew and Luke, Jesus assures the
disciples that "your heavenly Father" gives all that is needed. Now
his own teaching and performance of abundance confirm the limitless
generativity of the new economy. Thus the *parsimony of Judas* and
the *abundance of Jesus* provide an epitome of the larger struggle in
the Fourth Gospel between darkness and light, between evil and good.
The particular conflict between them indicates that the larger struggle
has an economic dimension in which his disciples are summoned to
participate. Judas assumed that there would be no more gifts given;
Jesus, the Gospel attests, is an agent of boundless abundance.

IV

Emancipation from the system of anxious scarcity takes place in
the Gospels not only through Jesus' announcement and invitation
and through his performance of the good news of divine abundance,

but also through the accent that he places on *forgiveness*. The petition for God's forgiveness in the Lord's Prayer understands that ready human forgiveness is the measure of divine forgiveness (Matt. 6:12; Luke 11:4). As Patrick Miller has shown, forgiveness is rooted in economic transactions, and the forgiveness of debts is deeply rooted in the year of release and in the Jubilee year, that is, in Sabbath writ large.[1]

The dominant economy of Jesus' day, presided over by Rome and practiced by those who accepted Roman authority, was an economy of extraction. That is why so much attention is given in the Gospels to the tax collectors, who were agents who helped transfer valuable possessions from those who produced wealth to those who enjoyed wealth. That economy featured an urban center (Jerusalem) that was organized and ordered by the urban elite who enjoyed surplus wealth. Many in Jerusalem were not among the elite and lived a subsistence existence. The elite who dominated the city depended on the labor of such subsistence workers, who are specified in the Gospel by the cipher "Galilee." Douglas Oakman has made a compelling case that the defining reality of this economy was debt, whereby subsistence peasants were kept endlessly and hopelessly in debt to predatory interests.[2]

Peasants who remain always in debt will eventually lose their land.[3] Of course this is an old story in Israel, as old as Pharaoh in Genesis 47:13–25. It is, moreover, as contemporary as today. Thus the *New York Times* reports on how investors make money by offering loans for cars to poor people at interest rates of more than 20 percent, which of course they cannot pay.[4]

The succinct social map of Luke 19:47–48 describes the social relationship of the debtor and creditor classes: "Every day he was teaching in the temple. The *chief priests, the scribes, and the leaders* of the people kept looking for a way to kill him; but they did not find anything they could do, for *all the people* were spellbound by what they heard."

The creditor class wanted to eliminate him, because he contradicted their socioeconomic arrangements. But the "people" were spellbound, and by clustering around him they protected him. They were, we may imagine, spellbound because he enunciated an alternative way in the world that was outside the protocols of persistent debt. When the text of the Lord's Prayer comes to the subject of debts and their forgiveness, both Douglas Oakman and Sharon Ringe make clear that the prayer has behind it the provision for the release of debt in the Old Testament (Deut. 15:1–18).[5] Those who make the petition thus state their readiness to cancel debts as a basis for forgiveness by God. Such a notion of debt forgiveness would in any case upend any conventional economy and disrupt the privilege of the creditor class; it must have been a welcome offer for the debtors, even as it was resisted by the creditors, who must have, in the rhetoric of the ancient text, appeared to be "hard-hearted or tight-fisted" (v. 7). The Gospel narrative is an interruption of conventional assumptions about the economy with enormous practical implications for the ordering of social power.

Thus, as we pray for forgiveness, we in fact petition that God will break the vicious cycle of coercion that keeps us all in hock, that we may come to the seventh day free of debt and ready for restfulness. There is no doubt that much of our violation of Sabbath rest is an endless attempt to come to terms with coercions in our lives, some of which are quite ancient and some of which are self-imposed, but all of which are powerful. That is why we must petition to have the cycle of restless indebtedness broken by the Lord of the Sabbath.

In Matthew 18:21–22, in the midst of teaching on church discipline, Peter asks Jesus about the number of times forgiveness should be practiced. Peter proposes the number seven, a good holy number that echoes the Sabbath. Jesus' answer, however, is seventy times seven, a clear reference back to the curse of Lamech (Gen. 4:23–24). And of course "seventy times seven" is not an exact number but means without limit, no curb on the capacity to forgive, no limit on the ability to break the vicious cycle of violence and indebtedness. This is Sabbath writ large. The teaching of Jesus summons a church totally situated in the practice of forgiveness:

> Put away from you all bitterness and wrath and anger and wrangling and slander, together with all malice, and be kind to one another, tenderhearted, forgiving one another, as God in Christ has forgiven you. Therefore be imitators of God, as beloved children, and live in love, as Christ loved us and gave himself up for us, a fragrant offering and sacrifice to God. (Eph. 4:31–5:2)

V

The emancipation performed by Jesus in the Gospels ultimately aims to constitute a renewed community with an alternative practice of faith that defies the dominant authorities through its orientation toward social solidarity. The Gospel narratives readily emphasize not only *forgiving* but also *giving* as central to that practice and that orientation.

1. In Mark 10:17–31 (Matt. 19:16–30; Luke 18:18–30) we have a narrative report that is divided into two characteristic parts, a public encounter and a critical reflection with the disciples. The public encounter concerns a man commonly known as the rich young ruler. He approaches Jesus with an expectation that Jesus knows the answer to the ultimate question of "eternal life." Good rabbinic teacher that he is, Jesus commends to him the commandments of Sinai. But then Jesus moves beyond the commandments to the requirement of his alternative economy. He bids the man, in five imperatives, to disengage from the conventional system of wealth, property, and debt: "You lack one thing; go, sell what you own, and give the money to the poor, and you will have treasure in heaven; then come, follow me" (Mark 10:21).

It is the additional requirement that marks the decisive break with conventional economics, which assumes that "treasure in heaven" does not require divestment of treasure on earth. Only so would Jesus then say, "Follow me." Luke Johnson observes that "Jesus demands complete renunciation of possessions for disciples" (see Luke 5:11, 28).[6]

The man had "many possessions" and found the break with conventional economy to be too much. In his reflective exchange with his disciples, Jesus states what they must have concluded: "How hard it will be for those who have wealth to enter the kingdom of God!" (Mark 10:23). The juxtaposition of "wealth" and "kingdom of God" makes clear that Jesus is after an alternative economy that is not preoccupied with wealth. By verse 27 the "how hard" of Jesus has become "impossible." The concluding exchange with Peter makes clear that life with Jesus is about abandoning wealth. Jesus does not say how the "impossible" becomes "possible," an enigma that is at the heart of an evangelical understanding of wealth and possessions.

That lack of clarity allows ample room for interpretive maneuver, but the clarity of his primary requirement is not to be explained away.

2. Luke 12:13–34 is partly paralleled in Matthew 6:19–21, 25–34, but Luke 12:13–21 has no parallel at all, and none of the material is in Mark. Again the text is divided into a public encounter and a reflective instruction to his disciples. The public encounter consists in an exchange of Jesus with a man who is in a dispute with his brother about family real estate. Jesus refuses to engage in his dispute. He makes two responses to the man's request. First, he warns him directly: "Be on your guard against all kinds of greed; for one's life does not consist in the abundance of possessions" (Luke 12:15). Ched Myers paraphrases: "You are not what you own."[7]

The term rendered "greed" means to grow bigger, to maximize abundance, to yearn for increase.[8] Jesus sees that the man is seduced to want more, even at his brother's expense. He understands that the man is using his energy for accumulation; he reminds him that the accumulation of more wealth cannot be the measure of his life.

His second response to the man is the parable of "a rich man," rich enough to have enough, owning land that produced abundantly His crops produce so much that he must secure more storage space. Recall that the Hebrew slaves in Egypt were occupied with building more storage facilities for Pharaoh's massive accumulation (Exod. 1:11)! The man in the parable anticipated that when he had stored more, he would be satisfied in his ample goods. That, however, is nothing more than anticipation that never comes to reality, because his self-congratulatory monologue about accumulation is interrupted by God (anything can happen in a parable!).

The man addresses himself as "soul" (*psyche*). But God addresses him as "fool," one who engages in self destruction by living against the grain of God's governance. It turns out that his great accumulation, designed to secure *his life*, led only to *his death*. Indeed, the question of verse 20 sounds as if he had no family or heirs, so that his accumulation had no future. His is a case not unlike that identified in Ecclesiastes 4:7–8. Finally, at the end of the parable Jesus makes it plain for his listeners by contrasting "treasures stored up" and "rich toward God"; "rich toward self" has no future in the presence of "rich toward God": "So it is with those who store up treasures for themselves but are not rich toward

God" (Luke 12:21). Jesus changes the subject on the man by bringing the issue of possessions into the presence of God, where they
are completely relativized.

His encounter with the man provides a case study for his instruction to his disciples. The man in the narrative is obviously "worried."
He does not have enough. His worry is propelled by his habitation
in a culture of extraction that assumes scarcity. The man is propelled
by a fear of scarcity. Jesus' disciples, to the contrary, are not to be
situated in an economy of extraction, are not to be preoccupied with
scarcity, and are not to be propelled by worry. It turns out that the
man in the narrative could not add anything to his life by worry about
more "things" . . . food or clothing. The man had lost his life (*psyche*)
by worry about surplus.

Now Jesus invites his disciples to reflect on the actual reality of
life (*psyche*) that does not consist in commodities or the accumulation of them. Worry belongs to a practice of accumulation paralleled
by a fear of scarcity. Such worry about scarcity is inimical to a world
where "our Father," the creator of abundance, governs. It is the Creator upon whom birds and flowers rely. These birds and flowers,
practitioners of abundance, are contrasted to Solomon, who, as we
have seen, was a practitioner of scarcity, accumulation, and greed.
There is a proper "striving" (v. 31), but it is not striving for wealth
and possessions; it is rather for the "kingdom" that defies the commoditization of creation.

In verses 32–34, it is as though the disciples had asked, "How do
we do that?" Jesus answers them: Withdraw from the world of fear!
The dominant economy is grounded in fear. The national security
state, with its surveillance and torture, aims to keep us fearful. The
mantra of scarcity tells us that we do not yet have enough. We have
not yet done enough. We are not yet enough! Television ads remind
us that we do not yet have the product that will make us secure and
happy . . . not yet. The antidote to such drivenness is to disengage
from such an ideology. "Sell your possessions, and give alms"! The
accent is on giving. The contrast is elemental: the man in the parable
never gave; he took. A life (*psyche*) of giving is sustainable; it is an
alternative treasure, alternative to treasures that erode, wear out, perish: "For where your treasure is, there your heart will be also" (v. 34;
see Matt. 6:19–21).

Jesus has masterfully managed the parable to contrast *commodity* with *creation*. Commodity is presided over by fear. Creation is presided over by the God who generously guarantees abundance. It is a stunning either-or!

At the end of the Lukan passage, it can be seen that the giving of alms is an act that profanes money, robs it of its sacred quality, and submits it to the rule of God, who is, as Creator, always generously giving.[9] The either-or, in the public encounter and in the instruction in discipleship, is, on the one hand, an exposé of a world governed by wealth and possessions, and, on the other hand, an invitation to alternative that is free from such anxiety-producing power. Discipleship is the renunciation of that anxiety-producing power; practically that renunciation is performed as generosity that is free of greed and has no fear of scarcity.

3. Finally, Luke's distinctive accent on the economic dimensions of the kingdom that Jesus announces and enacts is made even more explicit in the two parables of Luke 16. In 16:1–13 the enigmatic tale is preoccupied with "dishonest wealth," presumably wealth of the marketplace, which is at best transient. The penultimate urging is to be a sharp dealer about such wealth, but to do so in preparation for a time "when it is gone" (v. 9). The follow-up to the parable is the instruction of verses 10–13 that makes a contrast between "dishonest wealth" and "true riches." This in turn morphs into a contrast between "God and mammon" or "God and wealth" (v. 13). Thus the instruction that follows the parable seems to deplore preoccupation with market wealth and also to affirm that there is a very different kind of wealth that is to concern the disciple community.

The second parable in the chapter, also distinctive to Luke, concerns yet again a rich man who in his self-indulgence disregarded the needs of a poor man (vv. 19–31). The parable evidences Jesus' remarkable capacity to manage and utilize Old Testament traditions that live in deep tension with each other. The poor man is commended to Abraham, the carrier of God's unconditional promise. In the calculation of the alternative economy, the poor man is given unconditional attentiveness and valorization. By contrast, the rich man wants more warning to be given to his brothers who are equally rich. But Father Abraham is unresponsive to the request and does not extend such relief to the rich man or his family. Instead the rich man and his family are left to the tradition of Moses and the Torah, with its summons to a neighborly economy and its harsh sanctions for those who refuse such neighborliness.

Thus the map of social relations that is sketched in the tradition of Luke concerns exactly those with ample money and resources and those without such resources. Jesus exposes the fraudulent wealth as the world entertains it and anticipates a reckoning whereby such imagined wealth is seen to be a hindrance and not an asset. The result of such thinking is the devaluing of what conventional economics values and an insistence on an alternative valuing. Richard Lischer articulates the contemporaneity of the parable:

> It witnesses to the abundance of poverty in our own backyard among people we no longer notice. But in the ultimate fate of the rich man known to tradition as Dives (Latin for "rich"), it also teaches the poverty of abundance, for wealth establishes its own insulation from the poor and therefore contains the seeds of its own undoing. Dives cannot buy his way out of hell. The parable speaks to the well-off individuals and churches, which, though not exotically rich by Western standards, are insulated from the suffering of others by the many accoutrements of abundance. It is addressed to religious communities that have inherited the biblical language of poverty and lavishly appointed churches in which to talk about it.[10]

VI

The New Testament Gospels clearly and unmistakably portray the good news of the kingdom that Jesus announces and enacts as an extension of the emancipatory traditions in the Old Testament Scriptures that are inextricably concerned with the material conditions of life on earth and oriented primarily toward the arena of neighborliness that is the public good. Jesus offers a contrast to *the practice of scarcity* for his disciples whom he invites into his alternative kingdom of *God's abundance*. That abundance, Jesus attests, is grounded in the generative capacity of the creator God, who provides enough to sustain all life, which is, in fact, interconnected and interdependent.

The sacramental portrayal of that bodily solidarity is in the Eucharist, which is a meal of anticipation that voices the readiness to leave behind the old, failed world in recognition of the new world of resurrected life. The bread received in the Eucharist is broken, shared, and eaten in anticipation of a future that embodies all those who are broken, all those who share in the inexplicable gift of life. Participation in the "broken body" affirms that the giver of broken bread provides enough for all life, in order that we may live it in faithful gratitude to God and fully committed to the neighbor, especially the vulnerable neighbor.

We know Jesus' teaching that the commands from Moses to love both God and neighbor are the most elemental responses to God's salvation for those who strive to inhabit the kingdom of God. We are taught in 1 John 4:20: "those who do not love a brother or sister whom they have seen, cannot love God whom they have not seen." Thus we dare to judge that these two loves are in truth one love. The way we love God is to love neighbors in their fullness. Such love and neighborliness will well up in and through all who respond to and strive for God's salvation.

Questions for Reflection

1. As Jesus continues the work of abundance rooted in the Old Testament, his disciples do not understand. They are good with the details but not with the overarching significance of Jesus' teaching and actions. How have you seen this in your walk of discipleship? Why is it so hard for us to understand abundance and the new "governance of the bread"?

2. When we give in to the narrative of scarcity, it filtrates into all aspects of our faith, even into the Eucharist. This scarcity closes off the Table to many of our siblings. Have you experienced this before? Who are the people denied access to the Table in your own lives or churches?

3. We are also, through the actions and teaching of Jesus, called to forgive. This forgiveness is, at its core, understood in economic terms, as stated in the Lord's Prayer and shown in many narratives

of the Gospels. What does this forgiveness mean to you? Can the church truly live into this culture of forgiveness? How do we spread that message?

4. The teachings of Jesus speak not only about forgiveness but also about giving—giving that breaks the social structures that oppress our siblings and ourselves. What are you giving to yourself so that you can be who God created you to be? What are you giving to others so that they may be who God created them to be?

Conclusion

*S*o now some conclusions. I have walked slowly through ancient texts and narrative memories. But my purpose is not focused on ancient memories. It is, rather, to suggest that these ancient narrative memories are as contemporary and as urgent as our own life in the world now.

In various narratives and poems, the Bible presents a robust portrayal of salvation as an alternative vision of life in the world that is as distinctly countercultural and subversive of the dominant culture among us as it was of Pharaoh's Egypt. Many of us have been variously taught to misread the Bible, misconstrue the church, and misunderstand salvation as primarily an individual concern oriented toward another world and an afterlife. But I have emphasized throughout the materiality and economic dimensions of salvation in the Bible so that we may know better.

One must be alert to the risk of moving to our contemporary context too quickly without sufficient attention to matters historical and canonical. It is not possible, in my judgment, to "apply" the biblical texts directly to our own time and place. But, when we have done due diligence about history and canon, we can see how this ancient utterance helps us in our time and place to imagine alternatively when we are emancipated from the dominant assumptions of our culture. Thus contemporaneity concerning "biblical salvation" may help us to see that our present predatory economy (that depends on racist ideology, male domination, and idolatrous nationalism) is unsustainable, because it contradicts the purposes of God. Conversely we may see that while our present ideological passion seems beyond challenge,

God is at work evoking, forming, and legitimating alternative practices of a neighborly economy that is multicultural in its horizon.

It is clear, is it not, that the *kingdom of paucity* and its propelling ideology of anxiety are alive and well and aggressive among us. In the United States it takes the form of a national security state in which we are to be engaged in perpetual war—literal, ideological, and economic—in order to impose our will upon others, in order to claim the resources and develop the markets to our advantage. We are not inclined, or even able, to speak of the national security state frontally. Most often we speak of symptoms and consequences— racial injustice, sleepless nights, lost jobs, wounded soldiers, disabled economy—but we do not name and identify the core ideology that produces our social disability.

Our immediate experience of the *kingdom of scarcity* is our *entitled consumerism*, in which there is always a hope for more, in which those of us on top (or striving to be) imagine that something more will make us more comfortable, safer, and happier.[1] The ideology of consumer militarism is totally pervasive in our culture, fostered by a media that has largely polarized to serve the interests of its siloed constituents, by a judicial system that is committed to a national security state bound up in tribalism, by aggressive TV advertising that is simply a liturgical adjunct to consumer ideology, by a star system of performance and sports figures that invites all to a fantasy that is remote from any neighborly facts on the ground. The measure of commitment to that kingdom of scarcity is the force of credit-card debt that is designed to produce dependency and eventually poverty.

We may of course deny that our present world arrangement stands under such judgment. Such denial is likely when we absolutize our current ideology. We may of course despair that it could be any different; such despair is likely when we accept the legitimacy of our current practice and ideology. Our denial and despair, however, do not mean that the Bible's visions of emancipation and restoration are false. They only mean that we have not yet been *emancipated* enough in our practice of *imagination* to host an *alternative* that arises from the force of God's faithfulness. These ancient biblical texts constitute a means whereby our denial and our despair may be countered. They are at the same time resources for our truth-telling and our hope-telling that are grounded in the reality of God, who is in, with, and under these ancient traditions.

We have seen the Bible's alternative to the kingdom of paucity: the practice of neighborhood through a covenantal commitment to the common good. Such an alternative is not an easy one, because the kingdom of scarcity is totalizing in its claim. The biblical narrative, and much that is derivative from that narrative, is a sustained insistence on an alternative. That alternative is not easy or obvious or automatic. It requires a *departure* from that system of scarcity, an intentional departure, which the Bible terms "exodus." In the ancient narrative the Israelites did not want to go, and once they had gone, they wished to resubmit to Pharaoh. The departure is a piece of demanding, sustained work. The capacity to think and imagine and act and live beyond that system requires imagination that has dimensions of the psychological, the economic, and the liturgical. Indeed, the core liturgy of Israel (Passover) and the derivative liturgies of the church are practiced departures that now and then take on reality in the world.

While the matter is contested, I submit that theological study may well be an exercise in the art of departure, an enterprise that focuses upon the great traditions of critical reflection that are resources for thinking outside the box, for making decisions to be agents in our own history and not chattel for a system of production and consumption.

The biblical vision of salvation is grounded in a firm conviction about creation: the world is God's creation that God has called good. For the church, it is further grounded in our conviction concerning the incarnation, the confession that God has come bodied ("became flesh," John 1:14) in Jesus of Nazareth, who "went about doing good" (Acts 10.38) of a kind that is vigorously rooted in this world and the material conditions of our lives:

> The blind receive their sight, the lame walk, the lepers are cleansed, the deaf hear, the dead are raised, the poor have good news brought to them. (Luke 7:22)

I have no wish to deny any personal or otherworldly aspects to the Bible's vision of salvation, but I have no doubt that many of us need to redress our inattention to the material conditions of our common life when we think about salvation. In a culture that is determined to dismiss the claims of the neighbor and the neighborhood, a consideration of biblical salvation should empower the church with an urgent gospel mandate to develop disciplines and practices that emphasize good neighborliness as central to any faithful response to God's emancipatory work in the world.

Grounded in the biblical narratives and laws and the prophetic traditions, and in response to the acute current crisis of acquisitive greed, the church is, in my judgment, called to its public vocation to practice neighborliness in a way that includes both support of policies of distributive justice and practices of face-to-face restorative generosity.[2] I dare to imagine that the connection between this ancient textual tradition of public imagination and our current social crisis is pivotal for the faithfulness of the church. It is this textual tradition, like none other, that can lead the church to imagine (and practice) the world as a neighborhood network of mutual respect and concern, and not simply as a market of detached competitors.[3]

I imagine that this narrative journey from *scarcity* through *abundance* to *neighborhood* is the key journey that Jews must make, that Christians must make, and that all humans must make in order to be maximally human. That is the Bible's vision of salvation. And that narrative journey must be made again and again, which is why it is cast as a liturgy. It must be made again and again because the kingdom of scarcity has an immense capacity to nullify the alternative and to obliterate the journey. And therefore the journey must be taken again and again, lest we submit to the kingdom of scarcity, join the rat race, and imagine that living in a national security state is a normal environment for humanness. Such captivity of the human spirit must be again and again challenged, for it is that captivity that makes it possible

- to commit aggressive, brutalizing war in the name of democratic freedom
- to tolerate mass incarceration and acute poverty in an economy of affluence, most especially without an adequate health-care policy
- to sustain policies of abuse of the environment, all in the name of nurturing the economy

Captivation by the kingdom of scarcity requires us to live with unbearable contradictions, and we, except in our better moments, do not take much notice of the contradiction.

The journey from *anxious scarcity* through *miraculous abundance* to a *neighborly common good* has been peculiarly entrusted to the church and its allies. I take "church" here to refer to the institutional church, but I mean it not as a package of truth and control, but as a liturgical, interpretive offer to reimagine the world differently. When the church only echoes the world's kingdom of scarcity, then it has failed in its vocation. But the faithful church keeps at the task of living out a journey that points to the common good.

Acknowledgments

*T*hese pages constitute a continuation of the copyright page. Grateful acknowledgment is given to the following for permission to quote from copyrighted material by Walter Brueggemann:

Chapter 1: *Journey to the Common Good* (Louisville, KY: Westminster John Knox, 2010); and *Truth Speaks to Power: The Countercultural Nature of Scripture* (Louisville, KY: Westminster John Knox, 2013).

Chapter 2: *Journey to the Common Good* (Louisville, KY: Westminster John Knox, 2010); and *Truth Speaks to Power. The Countercultural Nature of Scripture* (Louisville, KY: Westminster John Knox, 2013).

Chapter 3: *Mandate to Difference: An Invitation to the Contemporary Church* (Louisville, KY: Westminster John Knox, 2007); and *Sabbath as Resistance: Saying No to the Culture of Now* (Louisville, KY: Westminster John Knox, 2014).

Chapter 4: *Mandate to Difference: An Invitation to the Contemporary Church* (Louisville, KY: Westminster John Knox, 2007); and *Journey to the Common Good* (Louisville, KY: Westminster John Knox, 2010).

Chapter 5: *Money and Possessions*, Interpretation (Louisville, KY: Westminster John Knox, 2016).

Chapter 6: *Mandate to Difference: An Invitation to the Contemporary Church* (Louisville, KY: Westminster John Knox, 2007); and *Money and Possessions*, Interpretation (Louisville, KY: Westminster John Knox, 2016).

Chapter 7: *Mandate to Difference: An Invitation to the Contemporary Church* (Louisville, KY: Westminster John Knox, 2007); *Journey to the Common Good* (Louisville, KY: Westminster John Knox, 2010); *Sabbath as Resistance: Saying No to the Culture of Now* (Louisville, KY: Westminster John Knox, 2014); and *Money and Possessions,* Interpretation (Louisville, KY: Westminster John Knox, 2016).

Chapter 8: *Mandate to Difference: An Invitation to the Contemporary Church* (Louisville, KY: Westminster John Knox, 2007); *Journey to the Common Good* (Louisville, KY: Westminster John Knox, 2010); and *Money and Possessions*, Interpretation (Louisville, KY: Westminster John Knox, 2016).

Chapter 9: *Journey to the Common Good* (Louisville, KY: Westminster John Knox, 2010).

Chapter 10: *Money and Possessions*, Interpretation (Louisville, KY: Westminster John Knox, 2016).

Chapter 11: *Mandate to Difference: An Invitation to the Contemporary Church* (Louisville, KY: Westminster John Knox, 2007); *Journey to the Common Good* (Louisville, KY: Westminster John Knox, 2010); *Sabbath as Resistance: Saying No to the Culture of Now* (Louisville, KY: Westminster John Knox, 2014); and *Money and Possessions*, Interpretation (Louisville, KY: Westminster John Knox, 2016).

Chapter 12: *Mandate to Difference: An Invitation to the Contemporary Church* (Louisville, KY: Westminster John Knox, 2007); *Journey to the Common Good* (Louisville, KY: Westminster John Knox, 2010); *Truth Speaks to Power: The Countercultural Nature of Scripture* (Louisville, KY: Westminster John Knox, 2013); and *Money and Possessions*, Interpretation (Louisville, KY: Westminster John Knox, 2016).

Conclusion: *Journey to the Common Good* (Louisville, KY: Westminster John Knox, 2010); *From Judgment to Hope: A Study on the Prophets* (Louisville, KY: Westminster John Knox, 2019); *Materiality as Resistance: Five Elements for Moral Action in the Real World* (Louisville, KY: Westminster John Knox, 2020); and *Truth Speaks to Power: The Countercultural Nature of Scripture* (Louisville, KY: Westminster John Knox, 2013).

Notes

EDITOR'S INTRODUCTION

1. The link is clearer in the German, *Gabe und Aufgabe*, which is the basis for Walter Brueggemann, *Gift and Task: A Year of Daily Readings and Reflections* (Louisville, KY: Westminster John Knox, 2017).

CHAPTER 1: EXODUS FROM EGYPT

1. I take the generative phrase from James Boyd White, *Living Speech: Resisting the Empire of Force* (Princeton: Princeton University Press, 2006).

2. See James Kugel, *The God of Old: Inside the Lost World of the Bible* (New York: Free Press, 2003), chap. 5, on the linkage between the human cry and the propensity of the God of the Bible.

CHAPTER 2: PLAGUES AND MANNA

1. See Terence E. Fretheim, "The Plagues as Ecological Signs of Historical Disaster," *Journal of Biblical Literature* 110 (1991): 385–96.

2. See William T. Cavanaugh, *Migrations of the Holy: God, State, and the Political Meaning of the Church* (Grand Rapids: Eerdmans, 2011), which offers a compelling statement about the political role of the church in the public world. Cavanaugh traces the way in which the "glory of the Lord" in the early modern period moved from the church to the nation-states. In my use of the term from Cavanaugh, I suggest that in the exodus narrative the movement was in the other direction, away from the kingdom of Pharaoh to the community of YHWH.

3. Michael Walzer, *Exodus and Revolution* (New York: Basic Books, 1985), 149, concludes his study with this sentence: "There is no way to get from here to there except by joining together and marching."

4. For a reference to Egypt's pyramids in an analysis of political/economic tradeoffs, see Peter L. Berger, *Pyramids of Sacrifice* (New York: Basic Books, 1975).

5. Erik Erikson, *Identity and the Life Cycle: Selected Papers* (New York: International Universities Press, 1959), 55–65.

CHAPTER 3: THE FIRST COMMANDMENTS

1. Patrick D. Miller, *The Ten Commandments*, Interpretation (Louisville, KY: Westminster John Knox, 2009), 117.

CHAPTER 4: THE CENTRAL COMMANDMENT

1. Peter J. Kearney, "Creation and Liturgy: The P Redaction of Exod 25–40," *Zeitschrift fur die alttestamentliche Wissenschaft* 89 (1977): 375–87; Joseph Blenkinsopp, *Prophecy and Canon: A Contribution to the Study of Jewish Origins* (Notre Dame: University of Notre Dame Press, 1977), 54–69.

CHAPTER 5: THE FINAL COMMANDMENTS

1. James A. Sanders, *Torah and Canon* (Philadelphia: Fortress, 1972), has seen that the canon of Torah stops short of land entry in order to serve the postexilic community of Judaism as it anticipated reentry into the land of promise.

2. Michael Fishbane, *Sacred Attunement: A Jewish Theology* (Chicago: University of Chicago Press, 2008), 119.

3. See the dense study of Augustine's analysis by Timo Nisula, *Augustine and the Functions of Concupiscence* (Leiden: Brill, 2012).

4. Adam Smith, *The Theory of Moral Sentiments* (1759; repr., Oxford: Clarendon, 1976). With an altogether different set of intentions, see also Jonathan Haidt, *The Righteous Mind: Why Good People Are Divided by Politics and Religion* (New York: Pantheon Books, 2012). Both Smith and Haidt long after him focus on emotive force in political and economic decisions, emotions that lie beneath and before the work of reason.

5. On the centrality of the neighbor, see Lenn Evan Goodman, *Love Thy Neighbor as Thyself* (Oxford: Oxford University Press, 2008).

6. Claus Westermann, *Genesis 1–11: A Commentary* (Minneapolis: Augsburg, 1984), 249.

7. See Walter Brueggemann, *Sabbath as Resistance: Saying No to the Culture of Now* (Louisville, KY: Westminster John Knox, 2014).

8. See Walter Brueggemann, "The Countercommands of Sinai," in *Disruptive Grace: Reflections on God, Scripture, and the Church*, ed. Carolyn J. Sharp (Minneapolis: Fortress, 2011), 75–92.

9. See Sandra Lee Dixon, *Augustine: The Scattered and Gathered Self* (St. Louis: Chalice, 1999), 142–47 and passim.

CHAPTER 6: ISRAEL'S LIBERATORY INSTRUCTIONS FOR ALTERNATIVE COMMUNITY

1. See Dale Patrick, *Old Testament Law* (Atlanta: John Knox, 1985), 63–96, and Frank Crüsemann, *The Torah: Theology and Social History of Old Testament Law* (Edinburgh: T. & T. Clark, 1996), 169–200.

2. Brevard S. Childs, *The Book of Exodus: A Critical, Theological Commentary*, Old Testament Library (Philadelphia: Westminster, 1974), 471.

3. See Marvin L. Chaney, "'Coveting Your Neighbor's House' in Social Context," in *The Ten Commandments: The Reciprocity of Faithfulness*, ed. William P. Brown (Louisville, KY: Westminster John Knox, 2004), 302–17; and Rainer Kessler, *Debt and Decalogue: The Tenth Commandment* (Leiden: Brill, 2015).

4. Elie Wiesel, *The Jews of Silence: A Personal Report on Soviet Jewry* (New York: Holt, Rinehart, and Winston, 1966).

5. Eugene D. Genovese, *Roll Jordan Roll: The World the Slaves Made* (New York: Pantheon Books, 1974).

6. Patrick D. Miller Jr., "The Human Sabbath: A Study in Deuteronomic Theology," *The Princeton Seminary Bulletin* 6, no. 2 (New Series 1985): 81–97.

7. Sharon H. Ringe, *Jesus, Liberation, and the Biblical Jubilee: Images for Ethics and Christology*, Overtures to Biblical Theology (Philadelphia: Fortress, 1985).

8. See Ellen F. Davis, *Scripture, Culture, and Agriculture: An Agrarian Reading of the Bible* (Cambridge: Cambridge University Press, 2009), 92–94, 108–10, and passim.

9. David Graeber, *Debt: The First 5,000 Years* (Brooklyn: Melville House, 2011), 390.

CHAPTER 7: NEIGHBORLY COMPASSION IN THE BOOK OF DEUTERONOMY

1. The term *paradigmatic* is used by Erich Voegelin, *Order and History*, vol. 1, *Israel and Revelation* (Baton Rouge: Louisiana State University Press, 1956), 12–22, as a contrast to "pragmatic," positivistic, "critical" history. For the same quality of Israel's tradition, David Weiss Halivni uses the term *pragmatic*; on his work see Peter Ochs, "Talmudic Scholarship as Textual Reasoning: Halivni's Pragmatic Historiography," in *Textual Reasonings: Jewish Philosophy and Text Study at the End of the Twentieth Century*, ed. Peter Ochs and Nancy Levene (Grand Rapids: Eerdmans, 2002), 120–43. For a broader consideration of these same issues, see Yosef Hayim Yerushalmi, *Zakhor: Jewish History and Jewish Memory* (Seattle: University of Washington Press, 1982).

2. See James L. Kugel, *The God of Old: Inside the Lost World of the Bible* (New York: Free Press, 2003), 109–36.

3. Jon D. Levenson, *The Hebrew Bible, the Old Testament, and Historical Criticism* (Louisville, KY: Westminster John Knox, 1993), 127–59, has warned against taking the exodus narrative beyond the claims of Israel and thereby dissolving its particularity. Levenson himself, however, acknowledges its legitimate usage in some derivative ways in other contexts.

4. On Deuteronomy as a vehicle of polity, see Norbert Lohfink, "Distribution of the Functions of Power," in *Great Themes from the Old Testament*, trans. Ronald Walls (Edinburgh: T. & T. Clark, 1982), 55–75; and S. Dean McBride, "Polity of the Covenant People: The Book of Deuteronomy," in *Constituting the Community: Studies on the Polity of Ancient Israel in Honor of S. Dean McBride Jr.*, ed. John T. Strong and Steven S. Tuell (Winona Lake, IN: Eisenbrauns, 2005), 17–33.

5. See David Noel Freedman and David Frank Graf, eds., *Palestine in Transition: The Emergence of Ancient Israel* (Sheffield: The Almond Press, 1983).

6. Older scholarship, typified by G. Ernest Wright, *The Old Testament Against Its Environment*, Studies in Biblical Theology 2 (London: SCM, 1950), sought to make the contrast between Canaanites and Israelites total. More recent scholarship has given much greater nuance to the contrast and shown the likeness between the two and the kindred reality behind the contrasts. Nonetheless, as argued in a more nuanced way by Norman Gottwald, *The Tribes of Yahweh: A Sociology of the Religion of Liberated Israel, 1250–1050 B.C.* (Maryknoll, NY: Orbis, 1979), conflict and tension are reflected in the text. Even the more recent accent on "folk religion" does not completely negate the sense of conflict and contrast.

7. Suzanne Daley, "After Harvest, Spanish Town Fights over the Leftovers," *New York Times*, April 3, 2015, reports on the contemporaneity of the issue of leftover crops in the field. Mr. Diaz judges of leaving the leftovers for the needy, "It's certainly better than having people go on welfare." Mr. Constantin concludes, "There are good farmers here and bad ones. Some of them say, 'Leave it all on the ground. It is mine.'" That contemporary dispute concerning leftovers in the field suggests the poignancy of the requirement in our verses.

8. Frank Crüsemann, *The Torah: Theology and Social History of Old Testament Law* (Edinburgh: T. & T. Clark, 1996), 234 (cf. 224–34).

CHAPTER 8: THE DYNAMISM
OF THE DEUTERONOMIC TRADITION

1. Karl Marx, quoted in David McLellan, *The Thought of Karl Marx: An Introduction* (New York: Macmillan, 1971), 22.

2. See Jeffries M. Hamilton, *Social Justice and Deuteronomy: The Case of Deuteronomy 15*, Society of Biblical Literature Dissertation Series 136 (Atlanta: Scholars, 1992).

3. Patrick D. Miller, "An Exposition of Luke 4:16–21," *Interpretation* 29, no. 4 (1975): 417–21.

4. David Graeber, *Debt: The First 5,000 Years* (Brooklyn: Melville House, 2011), 8.

CHAPTER 9: RESISTORS TO AND ADVOCATES
FOR BIBLICAL SALVATION

1. See Philip P. Jenson, *Graded Holiness: A Key to the Priestly Conception of the World*, Journal for the Study of the Old Testament Supplement 106 (Sheffield: JSOT Press, 1992).

2. I have suggested this parallel between temple and plane in "The Tearing of the Curtain (Matt. 27:51)," in *Faithful Witness: A Festschrift Honoring Ronald Goetz*, ed. Michael J. Bell, H. Scott Matheney, and Dan Peerman (Elmhurst, IL: Elmhurst College, 2002), 77–83.

3. For what follows on Solomon, see Walter Brueggemann, *Solomon: Israel's Ironic Icon of Human Achievement* (Columbia: University of South Carolina Press, 2005).

4. On such failed "wisdom," see Walter Isaacson and Evan Thomas, *The Wise Men: Six Friends and the World They Made* (New York: Simon & Schuster, 1988).

5. On the decisive role of the poet in the construction of society, see Walter Brueggemann, *Finally Comes the Poet: Daring Speech for Proclamation* (Minneapolis: Fortress, 1989).

CHAPTER 10: THE ECONOMIC CORE OF PROPHETIC CRITICISM

1. The best general study of the sociology of the prophets is Robert R. Wilson, *Prophecy and Society in Ancient Israel* (Philadelphia: Fortress, 1980).

2. See Walter Brueggemann, "Poems vs. Memos," in *Ice Axes for Frozen Seas: A Biblical Theology of Provocation*, ed. Davis Hankins (Waco, TX: Baylor University Press, 2014), 87–113.

3. Roland E. Clements, "Patterns in the Prophetic Canon," in *Canon and Authority: Essays in Old Testament Religion and Theology*, ed. George W. Coats and Burke O. Long (Philadelphia: Fortress, 1977), 49, 53.

4. See generally Claus Westermann, *Basic Forms of Prophetic Speech* (Philadelphia: Westminster, 1967).

5. D. N. Premnath, *Eighth-Century Prophets: A Social Analysis* (St. Louis: Chalice, 2003).

6. The basic study is by Klaus Koch, "Is There a Doctrine of Retribution in the Old Testament?," in *Theodicy in the Old Testament*, ed. James L. Crenshaw (Philadelphia: Fortress, 1983), 57–87. On the prophets in particular, see Patrick D. Miller Jr., *Sin and Judgment in the Prophets* (Chico, CA: Scholars, 1982).

7. This passage is of acute interest to me for a very particular reason. In September 2001, at the beginning of the semester, I was teaching a course on the book of Isaiah. By September 11 we had come to chapter 2; the class met just as we got news of the attack that day on New York and Washington, DC. The text, with its mention of high towers and fortified walls, seemed to the class and to me so immediately contemporary that it required almost no exposition on that occasion.

8. On the provisional "if," see Walter Brueggemann, *Solomon: Israel's Ironic Icon of Human Achievement* (Columbia: University of South Carolina Press, 2005), 139–59.

9. J. J. M. Roberts, *Nahum, Habakkuk, and Zephaniah*, Old Testament Library (Louisville, KY: Westminster/John Knox, 1991), 116–17.

10. See Paul Joyce, *Divine Initiative and Human Response in Ezekiel*, Journal for the Study of the Old Testament Supplement Series 51 (Sheffield: JSOT Press, 1989), 138–40 and passim.

11. The real affront of Sodom in the narrative of Gen. 18–19 is not one of sexuality, even though that is a popular assumption, but rather wholesale violence. Thus Ezekiel's allusion to the narrative may attest that "prosperous ease" and neglect of

Notes

the poor in fact constitute an act of violence not unlike the violence of Sodom; see Isa. 1:10, which voices a parallel allusion to the Sodom narrative.

12. Donald E. Gowan, *When Man Becomes God: Humanism and* Hybris *in the Old Testament* (Pittsburgh: Pickwick, 1975), 127.

13. See the extensive and persuasive exposition of this text by Ellen F. Davis, *Biblical Prophecy: Perspectives for Christian Theology, Discipleship, and Ministry*, Interpretation (Louisville, KY: Westminster John Knox, 2014), 119–33.

14. See Claus Westermann, *Prophetic Oracles of Salvation in the Old Testament* (Louisville, KY: Westminster/John Knox, 1991), and Walter Brueggemann, *Reality, Grief, Hope: Three Urgent Prophetic Tasks* (Grand Rapids: Eerdmans, 2014), 89–128.

CHAPTER 11: PROPHETIC HOPE

1. See Walter Brueggemann, *Reality, Grief, Hope: Three Urgent Prophetic Tasks* (Grand Rapids: Eerdmans, 2014), 89–128.

2. The "double portion" in chap. 61 may be an allusion back to 40:2, though the wording is different. More interesting is that the same term for "double portion" (*mishneh*) is used in Job 42:10 for YHWH's restoration of Job. That parallel may merit more study, for it suggests "twice as much" for restored Israel, even as it was for restored Job.

3. On the theological force and contemporary power of the book of Lamentations, see Kathleen M. O'Connor, *Lamentations and the Tears of the World* (Maryknoll, NY: Orbis, 2002).

4. Paul D. Hanson, *The Dawn of Apocalyptic*, rev. ed. (Philadelphia: Fortress, 1979), has traced the way in which competing voices of interpretation stand side by side in the text.

5. Rolf Rendtorff, "Isaiah 56:1 as a Key to the Formation of the Book of Isaiah," in *Canon and Theology: Overtures to an Old Testament Theology*, trans. and ed. Margaret Kohl, Overtures to Biblical Theology (Minneapolis: Fortress, 1993), 181–89.

6. The only other usage of this word for "eunuch" in Isaiah is in Isaiah 39:7, wherein the prophet Isaiah announces to King Hezekiah that his sons will be eunuchs in the Babylonian court. That is, the prophet anticipates royal persons becoming powerless servants in a foreign court. This textual reference in Isaiah 39 is important because it is the last chapter of First Isaiah, Isaiah 1–39. Our text in Isaiah 56, the other mention of eunuchs in the book of Isaiah, is in the first chapter of Third Isaiah, so that chapters 39 and 56 with their two mentions of eunuchs bracket the powerful poetry of Second Isaiah in Isaiah 40–55. This literary arrangement suggests that Isaiah 56 aims precisely at rehabilitating the princes of the Davidic house who had lost their power and their royal credentials, who had become powerless, nameless nobodies in a foreign court. They are nobodies out there, but in here, in restored Jerusalem, they are to be made welcome.

CHAPTER 12: THE EMANCIPATING IMAGINATION OF JESUS

1. Patrick D. Miller, "Exposition of Luke 4:16–21," *Interpretation* 29 (October 1975): 417–21.

2. Douglas E. Oakman, *Jesus and the Peasants* (Eugene, OR: Wipf & Stock, 2008); Oakman, *Jesus, Debt, and the Lord's Prayer: First-Century Debt and Jesus' Intentions* (Eugene, OR: Wipf & Stock, 2014).

3. See Oakman, *Jesus and the Peasants*, 140, on the dynamics of land loss.

4. Nicholas Kristof, "How Do We Increase Empathy?," *New York Times*, January 27, 2015, A23.

5. Oakman, *Jesus, Debt, and the Lord's Prayer*, 42–91 and passim; Sharon H. Ringe, *Jesus, Liberation, and the Biblical Jubilee: Images for Ethics and Christology*, Overtures to Biblical Theology (Philadelphia: Fortress, 1985), 81–90.

6. Luke Timothy Johnson, *Sharing Possessions: What Faith Demands*, 2nd ed. (Grand Rapids: Eerdmans, 2011), 15.

7. Ched Myers, "The Bible and Climate Change" (presentation at Society of Biblical Literature Annual Meeting, San Diego, CA, November 22, 2014).

8. The Greek term *pleonexia* was used recently to describe Vladimir Putin, president of Russia: "She [Masha Gessen] claims that Putin suffers from 'pleonexia,' the insatiable desire to have what rightfully belongs to others" (Tony Wood, "First Person," *London Review of Books*, February 5, 2015, 14). Of course what can be said of Putin can as well be said of the oligarchs who control the U.S. economy.

9. On almsgiving, see Gary A. Anderson, *Charity: The Place of the Poor in the Biblical Tradition* (New Haven: Yale University Press, 2013).

10. Richard Lischer, *Reading the Parables*, Interpretation (Louisville, KY: Westminster John Knox, 2014), 108. Nicholas Kristoff, "How Do We Increase Empathy?," observes that because the wealthy are effectively protected from an experience of the poor, they are much less likely to have any empathy for their plight.

CONCLUSION

1. See Daniel McGinn, *House Lust: America's Obsession with Our Homes* (New York: Doubleday, 2008).

2. William T. Cavanaugh, *Migrations of the Holy: God, State, and the Political Meaning of the Church* (Grand Rapids: Eerdmans, 2011), offers a compelling statement about the political role of the church in the public world.

3. On the agenda of neighborliness, see John McKnight and Peter Block, *The Abundant Community: Awakening the Power of Families and Neighborhoods* (San Francisco: Berrett-Koehler, 2010).